# Second time around

# Second time around

Campaigning reports from 2014 to 2021

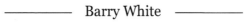

Barry White

Published by WaterMarx
The Grain Store, High Street
Urchfont, Devizes, Wiltshire SN10 4QH

Cover design Roger Huddle

© Barry White 2021
and individual contributors

All rights reserved. No part of this book may be reproduced or transmitted in any form or by any means, electronic, mechanical or otherwise, including photocopying, recording or in any information storage and retrieval system without permission in writing from the publisher.

ISBN 978-0-9570726-2-6

Printed and bound by CPI Group (UK) Ltd, Croydon, CR0 4YY

# Contents

| | | |
|---|---|---|
| | Introduction | 1 |

**Turkey**

| | | |
|---|---|---|
| 1 | Four journalists freed in Turkey | 3 |
| 2 | Erdoğan triumphs in local elections amid fraud claims | 3 |
| 3 | Turkish government criticised | 4 |
| 4 | Six journalists targeted by Turkish police | 6 |
| 5 | Odatv trials—more of the same | 7 |
| 6 | The trials grind on | 9 |
| 7 | Turkish authorities tighten their grip on critical media | 10 |
| 8 | Prison visit denied | 12 |
| 9 | BirGün trial adjourned | 13 |
| 10 | Turkish elections—despite winning, Erdoğan suffers humiliating defeat | 15 |
| 11 | Odatv trial—more delays; talks start on forming a coalition government | 16 |
| 12 | Planning the way forward in Turkey | 18 |
| 13 | After 92 days, Can Dündar and Erdem Gül are released | 21 |
| 14 | Outrage as court orders secret trial of journalists | 23 |
| 15 | NUJ speaks up for journalism in Turkey | 25 |
| 16 | Intimidation of free media in Turkey—we must tell the world what's going on | 28 |
| 17 | Botched coup gives Erdoğan the green light for massive purges | 31 |
| 18 | More trials pile up | 33 |
| 19 | The silencing of the media | 36 |
| 20 | Turkey's democracy is being frozen out | 39 |
| 21 | Odatv trial—after six years, is acquittal likely on 15 February? | 42 |
| 22 | The end of a farcical trial? Odatv trial: justice still denied? | 43 |
| 23 | At last, the Odatv 13 are acquitted | 44 |

*III*

| | | |
|---|---|---|
| 24 | UK report criticises Turkey's human rights record—but how will government react? | 45 |
| 25 | A divided country | 47 |
| 26 | Odatv update/two journalists face extradition from Spain | 49 |
| 27 | Some good and some bad news | 50 |
| 28 | Turkish courts refuse order to release two journalists | 52 |
| 29 | Conference calls for solidarity in action to help end repression in Turkey | 53 |
| 30 | NUJ condemns journalists' jailings; judge rejects extradition demands | 55 |
| 31 | Turkey—democracy denied, but not yet lost | 56 |
| 32 | NUJ member harassed and detained then deported by Turkish authorities for just doing his job | 58 |
| 33 | Erdoğan faces his moment of truth by challenging the results | 62 |
| 34 | Election rerun forced in Istanbul as Turkey heads towards dictatorship and economic instability | 65 |
| 35 | Erdoğan loses rerun of Istanbul mayor election | 66 |
| 36 | After Istanbul will it be business as usual? | 68 |

## Journalism and press freedom

| | | |
|---|---|---|
| 37 | Moscow revisited | 71 |
| 38 | After all this time—it's IMPRESS | 73 |
| 39 | Election 2017: Tories let press barons off the hook | 75 |
| 40 | It was social media what swung it! | 78 |
| 41 | Journalism under threat but not trusted | 80 |
| 42 | Press freedom plunges world-wide | 82 |
| 43 | Will the NUJ be the first union to recruit robots? | 84 |
| 44 | 21st Century Fox proposed Sky takeover—don't let Murdoch snatch victory from the jaws of defeat | 86 |
| 45 | Tory MP climbs down over the spy who never was | 87 |
| 46 | The Cairncross Review—can it reverse the decline of local and regional press? | 89 |

| 47 | Academic report critical of media coverage of Labour's anti-semitism debate | 92 |
| 48 | Murdered with impunity | 94 |
| 49 | No happy new year for them! | 97 |
| 50 | Public money needed to save local journalism says Cairncross | 98 |
| 51 | What sort of media do we want? | 102 |
| 52 | Urgent action needed to support public service broadcasting says Lords committee | 104 |
| 53 | Election 2019—Future of the media—what the parties say | 106 |
| 54 | Media reform—are the parties up to the challenge? | 109 |
| 55 | As Julian Assange edges towards freedom, investigative journalism takes a big hit | 111 |

## Mordechai Vanunu
| 56 | 10 years on and still not free | 115 |

## Durham Miners' Gala
| 57 | Banners held high | 117 |
| 58 | Tens of thousands celebrate the 135th Durham Miners' Gala—where campaigners highlight the proposed rendition of Julian Assange to the US | 119 |

## Election 2019
| 59 | The Tory manifesto—an Executive 'power grab'—we have been warned | 123 |

## History
| 60 | Under the Pennines and back in time | 126 |
| 61 | Angela's story—a unique life well remembered | 129 |
| 62 | Sensational election result in Walthamstow | 130 |
| 63 | An Inspector Calls | 132 |

## Plymouth Argyle FC
| 64 | To be a Pilgrim! | 135 |

**Pandemic**
65 Profit from pain ...                                      142

**Obituaries**
66  Geraldine Alferoff                                        144
67  Chris Bartter                                              145

**Climate change**
68  We have been warned ... again and again         147

**Acknowledgements**                                          151

# Introduction

This second book continues where my first, *On the Record*, left off. It contains a selection of articles and blogs written from 2014 to January 2021 at *www.thespark.me.uk*.

The first section contains reports from my visits to Turkey, made mostly on behalf of the European Federation of Journalists (EFJ), which I represented at trials of journalists, as well as by visiting journalists and other media workers whose freedom was under threat for just doing their jobs.

My involvement with the EFJ began in 2004, when I was elected for a three-year term representing the National Union of Journalists (NUJ). The EFJ is a regional organisation of the International Federation of Journalists (IFJ) and, like its parent body, is based in Brussels. The EFJ is Europe's largest organisation of journalists and represents over 320,000 members in 43 countries.

My interest in Turkey dates from my first term on the EFJ's steering committee (or board). I was part of an EFJ delegation which visited Istanbul and Ankara at the invitation of the Türkiye Gazeteciler Sendikasi (TGS), our Turkish affiliate. We looked at the restrictions on media freedom and the right to report, and discussed with journalists the problems they were facing from legal and other restrictions being placed on them, and how we could support them.

In turn, this mission led to the EFJ setting up its Turkey project, with funding from the European Union. Its aim was to support independent journalism, and offer solidarity with journalists facing imprisonment and criminalisation as a result of doing their work and supporting their demands for legal reforms to bring about strong guarantees for media freedom and the right to report.

I served a further two terms on the steering committee from 2010 to 2016, and it was during this period that I paid numerous visits to Turkey on solidarity missions, some of which are recorded in my first book.

Following the failed coup on 16 July 2016, the authorities launched a massive crackdown on civil society and more journalists found themselves the victims of state oppression. Under the state of emergency declared shortly after the coup collapsed, some 131 media organisations including three news agencies, 16 television channels, 23 radio stations, 45 daily newspapers, 15 magazines and 29 publishing houses were closed. President Tayyip Erdoğan used the failed coup as a pretext to clamp down on dissent and strengthen his grip on power. During the two years the state of emergency was in

*Second time around*

force Reuters estimated that 150,000 judges, academics, military officers, and civil servants were sacked or suspended. More than 77,000 people were jailed pending trial. The repression continues to this day with independent online and social media facing new censorship laws.

Latest figures (November 2020) from the Vienna-based International Press Institute record that 79 journalists are in prison, and that since 2016, 170 media outlets have been forcibly closed and 1,210 years of 'jail time' have been handed to journalists.

Many of these events are recorded in this book, which is dedicated to those brave women and men who tirelessly and at great personal risk to themselves, their families and friends, struggle to perform their role in serving the public with informed independent journalism, which is the bedrock of democracy.

One such brave person is the Australian publisher Julian Assange who at the time of writing is awaiting the outcome of his extradition hearing held at the Old Bailey. Assange, the co-founder of Wikileaks, faces charges under the US Espionage Act, which carry a potential sentence of 175 years.

Writing in the Press Gazette on 4 September 2020, journalist Peter Oborne warned 'that his case could have a devastating, chilling effect on journalism and the UK government has the ability to prevent this happening. Future generations will never forgive the current generation of journalists unless we raise our game and fight to stop the extradition of Julian Assange.'

Despite support from the NUJ there has hardly been a sound from the mainstream British press, although the charges pose, in the words of Michelle Stanistreet, the union's General Secretary, 'a threat that could criminalise the critical work of investigative sources'.

The rest of the book is taken up with reports, reviews and comments on events as well as more personal reflections and is broken down into subject sections.

Finally, I would like to thank colleagues from the EFJ, the NUJ and the now closed Campaign for Press and Broadcasting Freedom (CPBF) who helped with the publication of this book.

*Barry White*
*Settle, North Yorkshire*

*Winter, 2020/21*

# Turkey

## 1   Four journalists freed in Turkey
*7 January 2014*

**It's been a hectic 24 hours in Turkey with the welcome news of the release of four journalists, Tuncay Özkan, Merdan Yanardağ, Yalçın Küçük and Hikmet Çiçek.**
They were accused of committing terrorist acts in the Ergenekon case, in which journalists working for an online news portal, Odatv, were accused of being involved in a group (called 'Ergenekon') plotting to overthrow the government. (See *On the Record*, page 82.)
Özkan and the three other journalists were released on Monday evening (6 January) and have been united with their families and friends.
The releases were made possible by a change in the country's anti-terrorism laws, which reduced the maximum pre-trial detention period from 10 to five years. I will be attending the resumed Odatv trial scheduled for 1 April in Istanbul for the European Federation of Journalists (EFJ) and hope that all the charges against our colleagues in this case are finally thrown out. (The hearing was subsequently postponed.)
On his release, Özkan thanked the EFJ and its affiliates for their tireless campaigning for the freedom of journalists in prison.

## 2   Erdoğan triumphs in local elections amid fraud claims
*31 March 2014*

**Turkish Prime Minister, Tayyip Erdoğan is the clear winner in the local elections held yesterday.**
According to Turkish television, with about 98 per cent of votes counted by early this morning, Erdoğan's Justice and Development Party (AKP), in power since 2002, had 45.6 per cent of the vote. The opposition CHP trailed with 28 per cent. Some 50 million citizens voted.

Erdoğan set a defiant tone by declaring that he would 'enter the lair' of enemies who had accused him of corruption and leaked state secrets, saying, 'They will pay for this.'

Hürriyet Daily News (Turkey's oldest current English-language daily) today commented:

> Here is the naked truth: half of those corruption claims in any other democratic country would be enough for the collapse of the government: in Turkey it cost only some five points of loss in support of Prime Minister Tayyip Erdoğan's votes in the local elections on 30 March.
>
> It is also true that Turkey has not experienced an election with so much fraud claims in decades. Power outages in critical districts of critical cities like Istanbul and Ankara on elections night, replacing of poll box observers of the ruling Justice and Development Party (AK Party) during the vote count allegedly by street bullies to intimidate observers from other parties, especially in Ankara, trying to prevent poll observers from being in the room during voting, especially in the east and southeast of the country, are some of those claims.
>
> Those claims could have changed the result in some cities, but let's face the truth: the difference between the AK Party and others is not in the single digits. Istanbul and Ankara could have changed the picture, but it did not. The majority of Turkish voters have closed their eyes and ears to corruption claims, because Erdoğan told them to do so; he has still such an influence on them ...

*Hürriyet Daily News, 31 March 2014*

## 3  Turkish government criticised
### 31 May 2014

**On 30 May I contacted a journalist on the Turkish daily newspaper Zaman, offering a comment on the decision of the Financial Times (FT) to prevent the paper's journalist from reporting a speech given the previous day by Turkey's finance minster Mehmet Şimşek at the FT's London office.**

It is not the first time that Zaman, a major high circulation publication in Turkey, has been under attack by the Turkish authorities, as this article from the paper tells us.

> *Today's Zaman 31 May 2014:*
> The Turkish government has been strongly criticised by media circles after Zaman UK representative Kadir Uysaloğlu was asked to leave when Turkey's finance minister commenced a speech at the Financial Times' head office in London on Thursday.

Uysaloğlu said that only representatives of the state-run Anadolu Agency (AA) were given permission by the FT to attend Mehmet Şimşek's speech. He added that FT officials later allowed him to join the program, but shortly after Şimşek started his speech, he was asked to leave the room.

Speaking to the Cihan news agency after the incident, Uysaloğlu stated that FT official Wendy Wong told him that Turkish Finance Ministry officials had requested that he leave the room.

Pınar Türenç, president of the Turkish Press Council, lambasted officials for the incident and said the media had not experienced such restrictions in the past, adding that there can be no freedom in a country that does not have freedom of the press.

'It is not possible to accept a journalist, who holds a press card and represents a media outlet in another country, being kicked out during a Turkish minister's speech. Recently there have been attempts to restrict critical media in such meetings or speeches. I think this is not acceptable in terms of freedom of the press,' she added.

President of the Media Ethics Council (MEK) Halit Esendir, also expressed his frustration regarding the incident involving Usaloğlu. Recalling that Şimşek was giving a speech about investment in Turkey, Esendir said the incident is clear violation of basic freedom of the press and people's right to be informed.

'I am hoping that we won't experience such an incident again and I urge authorities to respect freedom of the press,' he added.

Also in April, journalist Tuğba Mezararkalı was told by Prime Minister Recep Tayyip Erdoğan to change her job and leave Zaman during a press conference. Prime Minister Erdoğan had told the correspondent from Zaman, which he associates with the so-called 'parallel state,' to leave her job while speaking to journalists at Istanbul Atatürk Airport before catching a flight to Azerbaijan.

This was not the first time Erdoğan had targeted Zaman reporters asking him questions on various occasions.

On 3 February, Erdoğan declared Zaman reporter Derviş Genç, who asked a question on corruption allegations after a major graft investigation became public on 17 December of last year, 'a speaker for the "parallel state"' during a press conference held at the same airport before a visit to Germany.

Another Zaman reporter, Ahmet Dönmez, was exposed to the same treatment during a joint press conference held by Erdoğan with Spanish Prime Minister Mariano Rajoy on 11 February. Becoming angry with Dönmez's questions, Erdoğan used insults against the Zaman reporter.

*Zaman was closed by the Turkish government under decree No. 668 on 27 July 2016.*

## 4 Six journalists targeted by Turkish police

*5 June 2014*

The European Federation of Journalists (EFJ) has criticised a new wave of violence against journalists in Turkey covering the anniversary of the Gezi Park protests—when thousands took to the streets and Taksim Square in Istanbul, to protest the demolition of the park to make way for a shopping centre.

Journalists covering the Gezi anniversary in Istanbul and Ankara have again been beaten, intimidated, insulted and injured by the Turkish police forces while doing their jobs. According to figures gathered by the EFJ affiliate, the Türkiye Gazeteciler Sendikasi (TGS—Journalists Union of Turkey), several journalists have been attacked by the Turkish police while reporting the peaceful protest taking place in Taksim Square and in the capital city, Ankara. They include:

- Ivan Watson (CNN): intimidated and taken briefly into custody during a live coverage for CNN International in Istanbul
- Piero Castellano (Italian photojournalist): injured by the police in Ankara
- Erdal Imrek (Evrensel): received tear gas in the face and has been beaten by the police
- Ahmet Sik (freelance, UNESCO 2014 Press Freedom Prize Laureate): beaten by the police
- Atilgan Özdil (photojournalist for the state-run Anadolu Agency): hit on the head by an unspecified object
- Meltem Aslan (journalist and trade unionist member of the TGS Ankara branch): beaten by the police who tried to get her press card.

The EFJ has said, 'Those police officers who were attacking journalists are acting with impunity, it only encourages them to continue to use violence against our colleagues.'

The TGS, which has called on the Turkish government to punish those responsible for the attacks, added, 'The government should have learned from its past experience and realised that attacking professional journalists, banning the means of communication and intimidating and threatening human rights defenders will never make the country a better place to live.

Reuters reported on the demonstration in the Guardian on 1 June. It described how the demonstrators were chanting, 'Resign, murderer AKP!' (referring to Turkey's ruling party) and 'Everywhere is Taksim, everywhere is resistance!'—before police, their helicopters circling above, fired tear gas into the crowd.

At this point, it reported, protesters with political banners fled downhill towards the Bosphorus Strait (the waterway that famously bisects the city of Istanbul).

Tourists were caught up in the events, and struggled to escape, many lugging their suitcases.

Turkey's Human Rights Association reported that 80 people were detained and 13 injured in clashes with police, although no official figures were immediately available.

CNN TÜRK reported that police also broke up protests in Ankara and the southern city of Adana.

At the same time, Sol Gazetesi (a left-wing daily newspaper), is experiencing judicial harassment for its recent media coverage.

*Sources: EFJ news release 3 June 2014. The Guardian http://www.theguardian.com/world/2014/jun/01/turkish-police-teargas-gezi-park-protesters-one-year-anniversary*

## 5   Odatv trials—more of the same

### 1 February 2015

**It is now over a year since the Odatv journalists faced their accuser in court (the last hearing was on 12 December 2013).**

The case, due to be held on 1 April 2014, was postponed. Although reforms to the courts resulted in the case being held under the new provisions, there we were, on 30 January, for the resumed hearing in the same Caglayan Judgement Palace in Istanbul, a short distance from the modern Florence Nightingale state hospital.

A change of court did not seem to change the predictable outcome. After just over half a day's hearing the three judges ruled that the case be adjourned until 12 June, five days after the national elections.

Spirits had been high as we met outside the courtroom beforehand. We had not seen each other for over a year. It was really good to see Muyesser Yildiz, the Odatv journalist adopted by the NUJ. She and her husband were as cheerful as ever.

The court proceedings kicked off just after 10.00 am with three new judges, and all the parties were introduced for the record. The

*Second time around*

lead judge made it clear that he wanted to complete the hearing today. Did this mean a judgement was likely today, I wondered? Of course not.

A computer expert (one of the country's top people, I was told) was called by the defence to give evidence that journalists' computers at Odatv had been hacked into from the United States, and hundreds of incriminating files had been placed on them. The presence of these files is a significant part of the prosecution case.

He was questioned by defence lawyers and the judge and, after 12 minutes, there being no more questions, he left the court.

The rest of the morning was taken up with speeches from the defendants and their lawyers. Muyesser Yildiz summed up the feelings of all the defendants when she asked the court to explain exactly where they were in the whole legal process, at the start, the middle or the end?

Others recalled their time in prison, and highlighted the contradictions in the terrorist charges they were facing. A defence lawyer called on the court to put an end to the case immediately. 'The defendants were set up,' he exclaimed.

After lunch, the court resumed for just over an hour, with more submissions from defence lawyers and for the first time the prosecutor spoke, towards the end, calling on the panel of judges to adjourn the case so that the court receive a report from the telecommunications company!

After a 30-minute adjournment we trooped back in to hear a statement from the panel of judges. The case would be adjourned until 12 June.

As we reassembled briefly outside the court no one was surprised at the decision. Disappointed yes, but these are hardened court attendees. And the significance of the resumed hearing being held just days after national elections was understood by all.

The ruling party, the Justice and Development Party (AKP), wants to win enough seats in the new parliament to change the Turkish constitution on its own. This would also include introducing a presidential style of government with, of course, the current President and former Prime Minister Recep Tayyip Erdoğan remaining in the top position with far more powers than he holds at present.

The judges, it seems, want to wait to see the outcome of the political contest before coming to a decision.

Separation of powers—I don't think so.

# 6   The trials grind on

## 1 February 2015

I did not only attend the Odatv trial (see 5: 'Odatv trials, more of the same') last week. The day before (29 January), I was joined by Mustafa Kuleli (General Secretary of the Journalists Union of Turkey, TGS) at the first hearing against journalists Can Dündar (Cumhuriyet), Utku Çakirözer (Cumhuriyet), Hakan Gülseven (Yurt) and Nazli Ilicak (BirGün).

The journalists are being sued by the President Recep Tayyip Erdoğan, his wife Emine and son Bilal for alleged violation of privacy and defamation following their reporting of corruption probes into Turkish politics.

A real family affair, it seems. As Can was speaking at a conference in Germany and could not be present, the case was adjourned to 26 March 2015.

The same day, I visited the offices of the daily newspaper BirGün where a number of journalists, including the Editor-in-Chief, are also facing serious charges and court appearances for their reporting. I told them that the EFJ was following with increasing concern the continued attacks on press freedom and the right to report in Turkey and will continue to support the TGS and stand in solidarity with our colleagues.

Two days later I met Editor-in-Chief Ekrem Dumanli and other journalists working for the Zaman newspaper, which was raided on 14 December. Although Ekrem was released after four days, Samanyolu Broadcasting Group Chair, Hidayet Karaca, who was also arrested with others working for the network, remains in Silivri Prison where he has been since 19 December. Both were arrested on the grounds of 'being a member of an armed terrorist organisation', 'depriving individuals of their freedom by force or threat' and 'false accusations'.

Meanwhile, according to a report by the Ankara-based Human Rights Watch and Assessment Centre (İHİDEM) on legal violations which took place during the 14 December raid, detainees, including Hidayet Karaca, were maltreated while in detention.

The report, which was released on İHİDEM's website a few days later, alleged that human rights violations took place during the government-orchestrated detentions of members of the press, including Zaman Editor-in-Chief Ekrem Dumanlı, Samanyolu

Broadcasting Group General Manager Hidayet Karaca and directors and producers of a popular television series. The report also said that during the detentions and court questioning, the detainees were subjected to treatment that is prohibited by the European Convention on Human Rights (ECHR), the Turkish Constitution and the Code on Criminal Procedure (CMK).

According to the report, Karaca claims police officers threatened and shouted at him, in addition to preventing his lawyer from being able to represent him properly. The İHİDEM report says Karaca's lawyers wanted to take photos of him for a statement, showing his physical and psychological condition, but were stopped by the police.

A US State Department statement made shortly after the raid warned Turkey not to violate its 'own democratic foundations', while drawing attention to raids against media outlets 'openly critical of the current Turkish government'.

## 7 Turkish authorities tighten their grip on critical media
### 20 May 2015

**Last week, a party from Samanyolu broadcasting group and Zaman met with Adam Christie (joint NUJ President) and me at NUJ HQ in London.**

Both media outlets are under government attack (see 6 'The trials grind on'). Metin Yikar (Samanyola) and Selcuk Gultasli (Zaman Brussels representative) together with Kadir Uysaloglu (Zaman UK) visited us to thank the NUJ and EFJ for the support we have given their journalists who face increasing pressure from the government. They also updated us on the situation facing Samanyolu Media Group head and journalist Hidayet Karaca, who was detained on 14 December for airing an episode of a soap opera that allegedly included encrypted 'signals' targeting an al-Qaeda-linked group.

They told us that, on 25 April, a court ordered the release of Karaca on grounds that there was insufficient evidence to keep him behind the bars (he still has not yet come to trial). The ruling outraged the government, which then jailed the judges who issued the verdict, and invalidated the court ruling, describing it as a 'coup against the government'.

Shortly after this, Karaca appealed to the European Court of Human Rights, claiming that his detention was unlawful and that he was not receiving a fair trial. Subsequently, he was transferred to a newly-built cell in Silivri Prison, some 60 kilometres east of Istanbul, without his family or lawyer being informed—a clear violation of the law.

Karaca, who has now been in prison for five months without any indictment, said on Twitter that there is no water in his new cell.

But there was worse to come with the news that an Ankara prosecutor allegedly asked the Ministry of Transportation, Maritime Affairs and Communications to forbid critical media outlets from using the state's communications infrastructure.

According to media reports, Ankara public prosecutor Serdar Coşkun, who is responsible for the Bureau for Crimes against the Constitutional Order, sent a document to the Turkish Satellite Communications Company (TÜRKSAT) Directorate General on 27 April, asking it to prevent a state-owned satellite connection being used by certain media outlets. This story has also been taken up by other newspapers.

Zaman newspaper says that 'The reason behind the controversial move, which has come shortly before June's general election, is allegedly the anti-government media outlets creating polarisation in the society and terrorising people'.

It goes on to say that, 'if the prosecutor's demand is carried out, opposition parties will be deprived of the means to conduct their campaigns and convey their messages to the nation for the June election, because most of the media in Turkey, which is controlled by the AK Party government, give little or no coverage to the election campaigns of the opposition parties.'

Meanwhile the Hürriyet newspaper (part of the Dogan Media Group) has also come under attack from President Erdoğan for its coverage of the death sentence handed down by the Egyptian courts to the former Egyptian president Mohamed Morsi in their 17 May edition.

Journalist Yosuf Kanli, the project coordinator of the Ankara-based Press for Freedom project, writing in Hürriyet on 20 May described the deteriorating situation in Turkey as follows:

> The rights and liberties climate of the country is getting worse. Media is so 'domesticated' with the climate of fear created by the government that mostly it cannot even dare report its own problems, while many media outlets and journalists have become lynch men of the government. The April report by Press for Freedom (PfF), [supported by] the Ankara-based Journalists Association, stated: 'The exclusion, alienation and discrimination against part of the press at the funeral of a savagely murdered prosecutor, at the presidency, ministries or the

commercial presentation of a company are crimes against humanity. Journalists cannot be barred from news.' Indeed, censorship reached such alarming levels that press cards are rendered useless, journalists are denied access to news or accessing news has become the 'privilege' of a 'select few' journalists serving with the media outlets loyal to the government.

In the first quarter of this year, 23 journalists and nine distributors were detained, one journalist was murdered and 10 were attacked. Three journalists and two caricaturists have been convicted of 'slander' against the president or his family. The trial of a 17-year-old student in Konya on grounds he slandered the president for using the slogan 'illegal palace, illegal' and the conviction of a journalist to a year in prison for sharing a message he liked on social media are 'shocking' developments presenting a bleak photograph of the 'advanced democracy'.

# 8 Prison visit denied
## 24 May 2015

**Last week I received official notice that my request to visit Hidayet Karaca, head of the TV media network Samanyolu had been turned down by the Turkish Justice Ministry.**

The news was reported in the 23 May edition of Zaman under the heading 'IFJ representative denied permission to visit journalist Karaca in prison'. The paper explained that the Justice Ministry had rejected a request from a coalition of international journalists' organisations to visit Turkish journalist Hidayet Karaca at Silivri Prison in Istanbul.

Mentioning me by name, the Zaman report says: 'Documents published by the private Cihan news agency on Saturday show that a judge turned down an official request from British journalist Barry White to visit Karaca, who has been imprisoned since Dec. 14, 2014, when he was detained along with dozens of others in a police operation against what President Recep Tayyip Erdoğan calls the 'parallel structure'. (By this he means the Gülen—also known as the Hizmet.)

Zaman explains that: 'White was to visit Karaca on behalf of the International Federation of Journalists (IFJ), the UK's National Union of Journalists (NUJ) and the European Federation of Journalists (EFJ), according to a petition signed by Ricardo Gutierrez, the Secretary General of the EFJ. The judge did not say why the request was rejected, citing only two articles of a law and a regulation that concern security measures in prison facilities and visits to the prisoners.'

Karaca was detained just three days before the first anniversary of massive corruption investigations on 17 and 25 December 2013, which implicated members of President Erdoğan's inner circle in the scandal. He is being held in Silivri Prison. There has been no indictment and no reason has been given for the extending his arrest.

Erdoğan (who was Prime Minister at the time of the arrests) denies corruption, and describes the scandal as a plot against his government by foreign powers and the Gülen movement.

The paper reported that in the December 2014 crackdown, 'Karaca and three former police chiefs were arrested on charges of leading a terrorist network, while other detainees, including Zaman Editor-in-Chief Ekrem Dumanlı, were released pending trial.'

*For background read 6: 'The trials grind on'.*

## 9   BirGün trial adjourned

*3 June 2015*

**In January I visited Barış İnce, Managing Editor of the daily newspaper, BirGün at his office in Istanbul on behalf of the European Federation of Journalists.**

He was facing charges of violation of privacy and of insulting President Erdoğan—the latter, which, if proved, could result in a heavy prison sentence. İnce had written an article entitled 'They lined their pockets twice,' in reference to a scandal about alleged corruption that involved President Recep Tayyip Erdoğan and his inner circle.

Yesterday his case came up in court but, according to Zaman, the trial has been adjourned until 22 October.

His story was based on records from the Foundation of Youth and Education in Turkey (TÜRGEV), a charitable organisation which was implicated in corruption. It lists Erdoğan's son, Bilal Erdoğan, and his daughter, Esra Albayrak, as executive board members.

In court, during his defence, İnce called Erdoğan a thief and, in a subsequent column 'Thief Tayyip' was spelled out with the first letter of each paragraph. The piece was widely shared on social media.

İnce now faces five and a half years in jail. The 'insults' he is supposed to have made were allegations of corruption against

*Second time around*

President Erdoğan and others close to him, which were made public on 17 and 25 December, 2013.

On Tuesday morning, several other journalists, civil society organisations and supporters attended the hearing—so many that they could not all fit into the courtroom.

At the hearing, İnce denied insulting anyone.

'I made a political criticism,' he said. 'I do not think that my piece was a crime. I am trying to defend my [initial] defence. It looks like I will be defending my defence this time [again],'

İnce's lawyer, Tolgay Güvercin, said, 'Barış İnce is being tried for news articles he has written. A journalist should be spat upon, not for writing about corruption, but for not writing about corruption. If we are not going to practise [law] according to the standards of the ECtHR [European Court of Human Rights], then let's all give up this profession, and we can close this court.'

'Barış İnce did not write the piece with the intent to insult anyone, but rather to defend himself. The criticism [the comment about the president] is harsh, but the suspicions about the plaintiff [President Erdoğan] have not yet been cleared,' added Ali Deniz Ceylan, lawyer for the BirGün daily.

Ceylan went on to say, 'We, as opposition media, are facing hundreds of investigations. But it is the job of the press to inquire on behalf of the public.'

Ceylan explained how Article 301 of the Turkish Penal Code (TCK)—which makes it a crime to insult the Turkish identity and state institutions—is being used to silence opposition.

Erodğan's lawyer also spoke during Tuesday's trial, declaring, 'My client is the victim,' to which the courtroom responded with laughter.

'The case is one of defamation,' he added.

In a written statement published on Tuesday, main opposition Republican People's Party (CHP) Istanbul deputy Umut Oran wrote that İnce is not alone in his fight and called on others to support him. Oran also attended İnce's first hearing last October.

*Source: Zaman, 3 June 2015.*

# 10 Turkish elections—despite winning, Erdoğan suffers humiliating defeat

## 12 June 2015

**Just two weeks before the 7 June Turkish general election, the New York Times ran an editorial on the subject.**
Headed 'Dark clouds over Turkey', it reported rising tensions in the country and that opposition supporters were fearful of a new crackdown to ensure that President Recep Tayyip Erdoğan's ruling Justice and Development Party (AKP) not only won the election, but increased its strength in parliament. An increase from 326 seats to 330 would give the government the two-thirds majority needed to change the constitution and turn Turkey from a parliamentary democracy into a presidential system headed by President Erdoğan. There were even fears that the election itself would be rigged.

Two weeks later, AKP's gamble failed when it got only 41 per cent of the vote and some 258 seats in the 550-seat parliament, well short of a majority. Second was the centre-left Republican People's Party (CHP), with 25 per cent of the vote (132 seats), while the Nationalist Movement Party (MHP) won 16.5 per cent (81 seats). The real winners were the pro-Kurdish Peoples' Democratic Party (HDP), which broke through the 10 per cent electoral threshold to enter parliament, winning 79 seats, some 13 per cent of the vote.

The writing was on the wall for Erdoğan two years ago, when the police brutally attacked peaceful demonstrators protesting at development plans for Gezi Park in the centre of Istanbul. They, along with protestors in other towns and cities, were physically attacked and denounced as terrorists and riff-raff. The lessons were not lost on what was becoming an increasingly radicalised protest movement, whose members clearly took their revenge at Sunday's poll.

Other sections of civil society were also concerned at the worsening events and the crackdown on dissent. Critical journalists and journalism were under constant attack during this period. Last December, the authorities struck with a massive police raid in Istanbul on Zaman newspaper and threats of anti-terror laws were used to shut down both Zaman and Hürriyet newspapers—the two main independent media sources—and their parent companies as well as on the TV network, *Samanyolu*.

So the electorate had defeated the danger of one-party rule for the time being, but multi-party politics has its problems: the parties opposed to the AKP do not agree on much and may not be able to work together in parliament. What's more, although the election should signal a reversal of the crackdown on independent journalism and dissent, there are many continuing trials and new ones in the pipeline.

Social movements in the country will have gained confidence following the election results—it's Erdoğan's first defeat, but they need to step up campaigns to strengthen democracy and freedom of expression.

It's not clear what Erdoğan will do next. Under the constitution, the role of president is supposed to be neutral, with power resting with the Prime Minister and parliament.

He will think otherwise, but he may be challenged by the Prime Minister and sections of his party angry at the election outcome. Having made the election campaign a personal matter and caused his party to suffer a humiliating result, he will not be easily forgiven by some. The shine has worn off, maybe for good—but never underestimate Erdoğan.

Power has returned to the people. Now it is the time for them to act to build a real democratic and diverse society so that there is no return to authoritarian rule. A tall order, but it can be done.

## 11 Odatv trial—more delays; talks start on forming a coalition government

### 17 June 2015

**I was unable to go to Turkey last week for yet another round in the Odatv trial, held on 12 June (see page 5: 'Odatv trials—more of the same') but the European Federation of Journalists was represented by Patrick Kamenka from France.**

The hearing was held in Istanbul's main justice palace and yet again the court decided to postpone the case (until 18 November) to get (yet another) technical report on the case, and decided to have it prepared by experts from Istanbul Technical University. This was because the defence believes that rogue files had been placed on the journalists' computers linking them to a terrorist organisation and sending them malicious emails.

According to an insider close to the defence, the report will be the fifth technical report on the case evidence. Previously, the suspects' attorneys had reports compiled by experts in Boğaziçi University, and Middle East Technical University, respectively. Following these reports, the court had also ruled some time ago to get experts from TUBITAK (the Scientific and Technological Research Council of Turkey) to write a separate, objective report on the case. They even ended up writing a second follow-up report, which caused the lead judge to say, that they, 'as judges, do not understand that much of technical stuff'. The court also listened to a technical expert invited to the court by one of the defendants' lawyers.

My source concludes that: 'If this was about justice, they would pursue the evidence uncovered in those (earlier) reports more aggressively. However, this trial is more a political witch-hunt than a case about an actual terrorist organisation. All they are doing is buying time until the dust settles in the political arena. If the dust does settle, they will probably rule in a manner which serves their best interests, and to whichever ideology that ends up on top in the current political hassle.'

Meanwhile, President Erdoğan has invited the largest party (the AKP) to consider forming a (coalition) government. Just after the election Prime Minister Ahmet Davutoğlu resigned in a procedural move after his AK Party lost its majority. President Erdoğan accepted the gesture, but asked him to stay in the post until a new government was formed. If Davutoğlu fails (unlikely—he has 45 days) Erdoğan is expected to invite the next largest party, the secular CHP to have a go.

Meanwhile pressure on critical journalists remains, with a Turkish court handing out a 21-month suspended jail sentence to an editor of a leading English-language Turkish daily newspaper after convicting him of insulting the President Erdoğan. The Ankara penal court said today's Zaman Editor-in-Chief, Bulent Kenes was guilty of insulting Erdoğan in a tweet implying his late mother would have been ashamed of him had she lived to see what he was doing to the country. Erdoğan's mother, Tenzile, died in 2011, and the tweet was posted in July 2014 when Erdoğan was serving his last months as premier, just before he won presidential elections that August.

## 12  Planning the way forward in Turkey
### 22 September 2015

**Increasing attacks on journalists, jailings, limits on collective bargaining, further restrictions on the right to report, more prosecutions and less press freedom ...**
These were some of the key issues discussed at a conference held in Istanbul on 17/18 September, 'Turkey: Fighting for journalists' rights and freedoms in a politically polarised country', which I attended and where I spoke on behalf of the European Federation of Journalists (EFJ).

The conference was organised jointly by the International Federation of Journalists (IFJ), the EFJ, the Journalists Union of Turkey (TGS) and the Journalists Association of Turkey (TGC).

It featured prominent speakers and panellists, including Can Dündar, Editor-in-Chief of Cumhuriyet daily newspaper, who outlined recent attacks on the media both political and judicial and gave the recent historical background.

'We discuss whether or not the press has ever been free in Turkey, but there has never actually been freedom of the press,' he said.

He referred to the harsh conditions under military rule in the country in 1980 and, fast-forwarding to the present day, said that, 'even then, I never saw a police state and fascism like this.'

He continued: 'One is free to write anything in Turkey, but have to accept the possibility that there will be a price to pay and sometimes that price can be very heavy.'

International Federation of Journalists' president Jim Boumelha reminded the conference of the impact which globalisation and the drive for greater profits also had on good quality journalism and pledged the Federation's continuing support for journalists in Turkey.

Andrea Schmidt (Second Secretary, Deputy Head of Section for Political Affairs, Press and Information) and a member of the European Union's delegation to Turkey said that they recognised, and were concerned about, the targeting of journalists by the authorities.

Other sessions included discussions on the work of the TGS during the past five years in campaigning against the jailing of journalists, while at the same time building their membership and signing new collective agreements; reports on attacks by the authorities on Kurdish journalists and media, especially in Kurdish regions; monitoring of journalists' trials and international solidarity; the need to build trade union organisation in the media; and the representation of women in the union and the media.

The conference also heard a description of the specific problems faced by Kurdish journalists and media following the ruling Justice and Development Party's (AKP) attack on outlets—when the former Vice Prime Minister Bülent Arinç described pro-Kurdish and two leftist newspapers as 'crime machines'.

Arne König, a former president of the EFJ, spoke about experiences covering journalists' trials and suggested setting up a wider coalition drawing in people from civil society to defend and promote freedom of expression.

In a session on Labour Rights I spoke about the importance of building trade unionism in the media.

'We also strengthen our professional and ethical standards when we have good workplace and trade union organisation,' I told the conference.

The conference drew up a series of recommendations and priorities covering action in the coming period up to the national election on 1 November and beyond.

These were later announced at a joint press conference, which outlined proposals for continuing to strengthen the union by building on the recent collective agreements with media employers and continuing to resist censorship and fight for freedom of expression and journalists' right to report without interference.

Following the conference, a delegation from the IFJ and EFJ with colleagues from the TGS visited the Dicle News Agency (DIHA) in Istanbul. According to the dossier they presented to us, the news agency website had, before 15 September, been blocked 17 times, making their websites unreachable in Turkey.

The dossier also highlighted attacks on journalists resulting in injuries, arrests and imprisonments.

The report concludes, 'It is worth reminding ourselves that for long years DIHA and independent Kurdish press have paid a heavy price for sharing the truth and will always continue to reveal and serve true news.'

*Outside Turkey, you can visit Dicle's website at: www.diclehaber.com/en*

Meanwhile, the European Union and the United States have expressed concern at the attacks on press freedom in Turkey and accusations of terrorist propaganda against critical media.

*Second time around*

The decision to open criminal proceedings against the Doğan Media Group came following allegations that its coverage of the fighting between government and the outlawed Kurdistan Workers' Party (PKK) amounted to terrorist propaganda.

'This is the latest in a series of disquieting infringements of media freedom within Turkey,' the European Commission said.

Doğan's Hürriyet Daily News was also attacked twice by a pro-government crowd earlier this month.

'We have been very clear about what our hopes and expectations are for Turkey, moving forward. It is distressing to see media freedom curtailed for any purpose,' said US spokesperson John Kirby, reported in the Hürriyet Daily News, in the weekend edition of 19/20 September.

The English edition of the same newspaper reported that the Istanbul prosecutor is seeking prison sentences of up to 26 years in a number of cases. These included Samanyolu Media Group Chair Hidayet Karaca (whose arrest is described in 6 'The trials grind on', which included details of my visit to the company in Istanbul in January) on charges of 'membership of an armed organisation, forgery of official documents and slander'.

The prosecutor's office also said that a separate investigation was underway into Ekrem Dumanli, a columnist and Editor in Chief of the Zaman newspaper. Samanyolu TV's chair was also detained in a parallel state investigation for alleged ties with Gülen movement—see 8, 'Prison visit denied'.

### *A crucial period*

Turkish society is entering a crucial period in the run-up to the 1 November elections. Journalists know that they play a key role in defending fundamental rights including freedom of expression and the right for the public to be informed and to talk truth to power.

The situation is best summed up by Serkan Demirtaş writing in Hürriyet Daily News of 19/20 September.

> In today's Turkey, those who are in government are trying almost every way to harass and silence independent media and journalists. A multifaceted effort is being conducted with the participation of the president, the government, government officials, judiciary, auditing institutions, pro-government media outlets etc. World history will surely mark this period in Turkey as the dark age of press freedom.

It is fearless journalists who are shining the light into the dark corners to prevent such a dark age becoming a reality.

*For further details of the conference go to the EFJ web site at: www.europeanjournalists.org*

and for the conference conclusions go to:
*http://www.ifj.org/fileadmin/images/Europe/turkey/Istanbul_co
nclusions_PR-1.docx*

## 13 After 92 days, Can Dündar and Erdem Gül are released

*27 February 2016*

**At last, better news from Turkey. Turkey's Constitutional Court ruled on 25 February that the rights of Cumhuriyet newspaper's editor-in-chief Can Dündar and chief of its Ankara bureau Erdem Gül had been violated.**

The ruling highlighted violations of Article 19 (right to personal liberty and security), Article 26 (freedom of expression) and Article 28 (press freedom) in Turkey's Constitution. The Court voted for their release by 12 votes to three. It could mark a return to the rule of law in Turkey and sets a promising example for other similar cases.

Dündar and Gül were arrested on 26 November 2015, following the publication of a story in their newspaper in May, which said that Turkey was sending arms to Islamic rebels in Syria.

The story was based on a 2014 video, which was reported as showing the country's state intelligence agency helping to transport weapons to Syria.

It was admitted that the lorries, which were stopped by the Turkish paramilitary forces and police officers en route to the Syrian border, did indeed belong to the intelligence agency. But President Erdoğan, who was furious at the revelations, said they were carrying aid to Turkmen rebels in Syria who, it seems, were fighting both Isis and the Syrian regime, led by President Assad.

Dündar and Gül still face aggravated life sentences, an additional life sentence, as well as 30 years in prison for revealing state secrets in their May 2015 report. Their trial opens in Istanbul on 25 March and I will be representing the International Federation of Journalists/European Federation of Journalists (IFJ/EFJ) at the hearing.

The release was welcomed by the IFJ/EFJ who, along with others, have vigorously campaigned for it. The Organisation for Security and Co-operation in Europe (OSCE) Representative on Freedom of the Media, Dunja Mijatović, also welcomed the release, commenting: 'The release marks an important day for media freedom in Turkey, but the charges against Dündar and Gül must be dropped, and Turkey must embark upon the reform of the laws that can currently criminalise journalistic work.'

A strong local and international campaign from journalists, trade unionists and press freedom organisations has been very active and effective since the arrests.

The TGS (Turkish Journalists Union) said: 'The Constitutional Court has ruled that our friends were not arrested for espionage but for carrying out journalistic activities. In this respect, the decision will leave a mark on history.'

Welcoming the release, the EFJ/IFJ is now calling on the authorities to drop all the charges against them and to release the other 30 journalists still in jail.

This followed a visit from a delegation that included European TUC General Secretary Luca Visentini and International TUC Deputy General Secretary Jaap Wienen, along with their Turkish affiliate DISK to the Silivri Prison, west of Istanbul, where the journalists were held, and from where they had called for their immediate release.

'This [release] is a victory for justice and freedom of the press,'

After 92 days, Can Dündar and Erdem Gül are released. From left to right, Süleyman Çelebi (CHP member of parliament, former president of DİSK), Hasan Cemal (journalist), Dilek Dündar and Can Dündar.

said Luca Visentini, 'and a victory for the Turkish trade unions who worked so hard to publicise their case. Trade unions have a vital role to play in the development of Turkey into a strong democracy and an economic powerhouse. It is to Turkey's credit that the Constitutional

Court took this decision and I hope the Turkish authorities welcome and respect it.'

Wienen added: 'With dozens more journalists still in prison in Turkey, this decision from the Constitutional Court in support of press freedom should pave the way for the release of the other journalists, too.'

## 14  Outrage as court orders secret trial of journalists

### 28 March 2016

**Friday 25 March was a bleak day for Turkish journalism, the rule of law and the public's right to know, when an Istanbul court ruled that the entire trial of Can Dündar and Erdem Gül should be held behind closed doors.**

The two journalists face charges of espionage, aiding a terrorist organisation, disclosing classified documents and reporting the supply of weapons to rebels in Syria by the Turkish security services. They could face life imprisonment if found guilty. The case resumes on 1 April.

Earlier, scores of their supporters arrived at the court to show their solidarity with the journalists. I was among them. As we gathered outside the courtroom, proceedings were suddenly switched to another courtroom on the floor below, which had more space. However it still could not accommodate us all and I finally got a place in the court some 30 minutes after the proceedings had started.

Two issues needed to be sorted out before the trial proper could begin. Firstly, President Erdoğan and the MIT (the National Intelligence Agency) had asked to be legally represented at the hearings. Secondly, and more disturbing, but not surprising, was a request from the new prosecutor, who had been given the case just two days ago, that the hearings should be held in secret, as classified documents were involved and members of the security services might be called as witnesses.

At 11.30 am, the three (male) judges retired to consider the applications. Half an hour later they returned to announce that they had granted both requests. The decision was greeted with boos and catcalls from those members of the public who had managed to get in. We were then told to leave before further proceedings could take place.

Foreign diplomats, observers from foreign press freedom organisations and NGOs, deputies from the Turkish parliament along with other members of the public left the courtroom, many at a snail's pace, much to the annoyance of the court officials. Before leaving I spoke to Can Dündar, saying that we in the IFJ/EFJ were with them 'all the way'.

Our hosts in Istanbul, the Journalists Union of Turkey (TGS) had hired a lawyer, who we met the night before, to represent the union's interests in the case. He was also told by the Court that he could not attend any further hearings.

However he was able to report that both defendants were allowed to leave the court, following the earlier ruling by the Turkish Constitutional Court on 26 February that they should be released after 92 days' imprisonment—despite President Erdoğan's outburst at the decision that he 'did not respect the Constitutional Court ruling' and that they might be returned to prison (see 13 'After 92 days, Can Dündar and Erdem Gül are released'). Those fears are unfounded for the moment.

The next day I read in the English language paper, Hürriyet Daily News, that some lawyers had refused to leave the courtroom after the judges rejected their request to follow the hearings. The court then decided to file a criminal complaint against them for 'obstructing justice'.

The evening before the trial, national and international media unions and professional organisations held a press conference in Istanbul to demand freedom of information and freedom of journalists. International organisations explained the actions they had taken and how they would continue to support the campaign for journalists and press freedom. Can Dündar and Erdem Gül also spoke.

In my contribution I quoted a letter from the UK Foreign and Commonwealth Office on actions the UK government had taken with the Turkish authorities over the need for press freedom and other human rights.

I also reported on recent activities by the IFJ/EFJ in Brussels and details of these may be found on the IFJ and EFJ websites.

I concluded by saying that 'There are those in this society who promote fear as a tool of censorship and repression. Let us counter that with hope which is the fuel of progress and remember that fear is the prison in which we put ourselves.'

*IFJ and EFJ websites are at:*
*http://www.ifj.org/ and http://europeanjournalists.org/*

## 15  NUJ speaks up for journalism in Turkey

*18 April 2016*

The worsening situation in Turkey was discussed at the NUJ Delegate Meeting this weekend in Southport (14—17 April).

Among a number of excellent motions was one from Cambridge branch: a comprehensive late notice (emergency) motion covering recent developments in the trial of Can Dündar and Erdem Gül. (Their case comes up again next week in the Istanbul court.)

The motion urged NUJ members to 'speak up for our persecuted brothers and sisters in Turkey', and asked that these issues be taken up with the NUJ Parliamentary Group.

Reference was also made to the Odatv trial, which has dragged on for five years. There had been a further hearing on the Odatv case on 13 April, at which the expert report on the issue was positive concerning evidence that incriminating material was planted on the Odatv office computers. The next hearing was scheduled for 21 September.

Another motion highlighted the case of two Vice News journalists and their local adviser Mohammed Rasool. Last August, they were arrested and held by the Turkish authorities while reporting on the conflicts between Kurdish activists and the Turkish military in the south-east of Turkey. Following a national and international campaign, the journalists were released after 11 days, but Mohammed remained in captivity until 5 January 2016, when he, too, was finally released on bail.

I also updated my EFJ report to the delegate meeting on the IFJ/EFJ Turkey campaign. The EFJ will be holding its general meeting on 25—26 April in Sarajevo. It will be my last meeting, as I leave the EFJ steering committee (board), having served the maximum nine years allowed under the rules.

### *Muhammed Zahir al Shurgat*

On 13 April, media freedom campaigners reported how Syrian journalist Muhammed Zahir al Shurgat died of his wounds after being shot in the head on Sunday by a masked ISIS gunman in southern Turkey.

The International and European Federations of Journalists condemned the killing and demanded that the Turkish authorities investigate the murder and act to ensure the safety of other journalists.

The ISIS-affiliated news agency, Amaq, reported that 'a security detachment that belongs to ISIS' shot Zahir al Shurgat, who worked at the Aleppo Today TV channel. Reports claim an ISIS gunman shot him in the head with a silenced pistol outside his workplace in Gaziantep, located near the border with Syria. He was rushed to hospital in a critical condition but later died of his wounds.

More at:

http://www.ifj.org/nc/news-single-view/backpid/50/article/turkey-syrian-journalist-reportedly-killed-by-isis/

### Erdem Gül and Can Dündar

I had written earlier to Hilary Benn (Shadow Foreign Secretary) and to Foreign Secretary Philip Hammond in early February about their case. The reply from the Foreign Office was as follows:

> The UK shares your concerns over freedom of the press in Turkey as does the Council of Europe, the Organisation for Security and Cooperation in Europe and the European Commission. We believe that freedom of expression must be respected and all media outlets must be allowed to report freely.
>
> We strongly encourage Turkey to continue (to) work towards the full protection of fundamental rights, especially in the areas of minority rights, freedom of religion and freedom of expression. We welcome progress made thus far and as the EU Commission highlights further sustained work is needed to meet EU standards.
>
> We continue to underline the importance of freedom of expression and all fundamental freedoms as part of our broader dialogue with the Turkish government. Our Ambassador in Ankara highlighted his concerns about the number of journalists detained in Turkey, including Mr Dündar and Mr Gül, in his public blog released on International Human Rights day. The Prime Minister underlined the importance of protections for a free press and human rights to Prime Minister Davutoglu when they met on 7 March.
>
> The Foreign Secretary set out the UK's concerns on freedom of expression when he met his counterpart on 12 March. The Minister for Europe also discussed media freedoms and rule of law issues with Deputy Prime Minister Simsek on 12 March. *(See http://thespark.me.uk/?p=654)*

### Turkish government demands prosecution of German comedian

The Turkish government has demanded the prosecution under German law of Germany's most popular comedian, Jan Böhmermann, over a satirical poem he read on German television in which he called Turkish President Erdoğan a 'goat-f*****' and described him as watching child pornography.

The comedian could face up to five years in prison.

According to the New York Times, Böhmermann is to be prosecuted under Article 103, a German lèse-majesté law that prohibits insulting a foreign head of state. Passed in 1871, it has been used to silence critics of Shah Mohammed Reza Pahlavi of Iran and the Chilean dictator Augusto Pinochet. It allows prosecution in Germany only with the consent of the government.

The Turkish demand presented Chancellor Angela Merkel with a dilemma: she could either compromise on cherished German values of free speech or risk relations with a leader she needs to prevent another influx of refugees. On Friday she chose the former, and announced that the German Federal Government would authorise the comedian's prosecution.

The DJV (Deutscher Journalisten-Verband) and Dju in ver.di (Deutsche Journalistinnen und Journalisten Union in ver.di) (EFJ affiliates in Germany) criticised the German Chancellor's decision. The DJV chair, Frank Überall, believes it sends the wrong signals to the Turkish government.

'The situation is even worse since press freedom is not respected in Turkey,' he said, and added that the Chancellor's decision was not offset by the fact that she has previously addressed the massive violations of the press and freedom of expression in Turkey.

He did, however, add his approval over the fact that the Chancellor was seeking the abolition of Article 103.

Dju in ver.di was also clear that Merkel should have objected to this decision to prosecute.

The EFJ also condemned the recent blocking by Turkey's telecommunications authority (TIB) of the website belonging to Sputnik, the Russian news agency.

'Turkish authorities cannot use administrative decisions to block access to news sites. Those measures are attacking Turkey's public rights to access information,' said an EFJ spokesperson.

**More at:**
*http://europeanjournalists.org/blog/2016/04/15/germany-prosecutes-a-comedian-on-turkeys-request/*

**Update:**
*In October 2016, prosecutors dropped the case against Böhmermann on the grounds of 'insufficient evidence'.*

## 16 Intimidation of free media in Turkey—we must tell the world what's going on

### 29 June 2016/October 2020

**Turkish journalists Can Dündar and Erdem Gül have called on journalists to publicise the truth about what is happening to the shrinking free media in Turkey.**

Can Dündar, Cumhuriyet's Editor-in-Chief was recently sentenced to five years and 10 months and his colleague, Gül to five years, for spying, aiding terrorism, attempting to topple the government and revealing state secrets (that the intelligence services were trafficking arms to Syria to radical Islamic groups). Can Dündar—whose passport has been returned, pending an appeal that could take over a year—was speaking on 29 June to a London meeting called by English PEN, in partnership with the Centre for Turkey Studies in London. He explained the background to the case against himself and Erdem Gül in a talk that formed part of a tour of European cities aimed at publicising their cases and those of dozens of other journalists who face censorship and prison.

Although the first session of the trial held on 25 March (see 14 'Outrage as court orders secret trial of journalists') was held in public, later sessions were held in secret. Following the session held at the main Istanbul court in May, when the sentences were handed down, Can survived an attack by a gunman, who fired at him outside the court building. His wife, Dilek, who grabbed the gunman, also attended the London meeting with their son, Ege Dündar.

At the 29 June talk, Can went on to report recent developments in the case of Şebnem Korur Fincancı, President of Turkey Human Rights Foundation, Erol Önderoğlu, a journalist with the IPS Communication Foundation (Bianet) since 1995 and RSF correspondent since 1996 and Ahmet Nesin, a journalist and writer. This involved the arrest on 20 June of the three, along with acting Editor-in-Chief of the Kurdish daily newspaper Özgür Gündem (meaning 'Free Agenda'). They were arrested for participating in the solidarity campaign launched by the Diyarbakir-based Association of Free Journalists for Özgür Gündem, which is known for its coverage of Kurdish issues and the decades-long conflict between the Turkish army and the PKK (Kurdistan Workers' Party). The PKK seeks Kurdish autonomy, but the Turkish government considers it a terrorist organisation.

Following the update, the meeting discussed the deteriorating situation in Turkey, where over 30 journalists are in jail and up to 2,000 people, many of them journalists, face charges of insulting the president. There was an urgent need for the international community to exert pressure on President Erdoğan, who controls over 80 per cent of the media in Turkey.

Ways of improving links between journalists in the UK and Turkey were examined, in order to better expose the attacks on free speech and the right to report. The need to build solidarity with other professions under attack was stressed.

We heard that the entire fabric of civil society in Turkey was getting weaker, with the government also tightening its grip on the army and judiciary. Ways to develop links with Turkish and Kurdish groups, especially in London, were also discussed.

## *Westminster meeting*

In the evening, Can Dündar spoke to a packed meeting in Westminster, called by the Centre for Turkey Studies and chaired by Lord Jeremy Purvis of Tweed.

Can Dündar opened his remarks by offering condolences to families and friends who had suffered in the terror attack at Istanbul's Atatürk Airport the previous day. Then, in a powerful and well-received presentation, he reminded the meeting that he had been a journalist for nearly forty years in both TV and newspapers and journalism 'had never been so hellish as it is now'. It had been his first time in prison and the first time he had been attacked by a gunman. Now Turkey has the highest proportion of its journalists in the world in prison, surpassing China.

Can Dündar went on to talk about the attacks by the Justice and Development Party (AKP) and its leader President Erdoğan on western republican and secular values in Turkey. These were established in the early 1920s by Kamal Atatürk, after the collapse of the Ottoman Empire.

He was critical of the March agreement between the EU and President Erdoğan, which had resulted in Turkey protecting European borders by keeping out refugees who were fleeing war and oppression. He believed that, in giving financial aid to Turkey and considering the possibility of visa free-travel to some EU countries, the European Commission had abandoned its commitments to human rights in Turkey.

He concluded by saying that fear was the greatest enemy in the struggle, and called on the West to stop Turkey sliding into a fascist state.

In the following question and answer session, Dündar described the financial crisis facing what was left of the free media and the impact on society of the extensive government control over the media, army and judiciary. This, coupled with the weakening of civil society, highlighted the need for greater international solidarity and support.

In reply to questions, he spoke passionately about the Kurdish struggle, arguing for peace talks and negotiations and described the state of the opposition in Turkey as 'very difficult'.

He called again on the western media to step up their efforts to draw attention to these issues in order to isolate Erdoğan and show the Turkish communities abroad the true nature of his despotic rule.

*A fuller report on the Westminster meeting can be found on the Centre for Turkey Studies website at:*
*http://ceftus.org/2016/07/01/westminster-debate-with-can-dundar-quo-vadis-turkiye/*

**Update**
*On 6 May 2016, there was a failed assassination attempt on Can Dündar in the car park in front of the Istanbul courthouse where he had been defending himself against the charges brought against him. The assailant was foiled by his wife, Dilek, and an MP. Dündar was unhurt, but a journalist walking with him suffered a leg injury. The assailant was taken into custody. Later that day, Can Dündar was sentenced to five years and 10 months for 'leaking secret information of the state'.*

*He later moved to Germany (before the sentence could be carried out) and in August stepped down as Editor-in-Chief of* Cumhuriyet, s*tating that he would continue as a columnist for the newspaper. An arrest warrant in absentia was issued in Turkey for him on 31 October 2016. He continues to live in Germany with Dilek.*

*In July 2018 Erdem Gül was acquitted of charges of 'publishing state secrets' and was elected mayor of Princes' Islands (South East of Istanbul) for the Republican People's Party (CHP)in 2019.*

*In October 2020, Can Dündar was effectively exiled when an Istanbul court declared him a fugitive of justice and ordered that his assets be seized. He had been given 15 days to return to Turkey but declined. The court then ordered the seizure of properties belonging to him as well as bank accounts in his name.*

## 17 Botched coup gives Erdoğan the green light for massive purges
### 20 July 2016/November 2020

**The failure of the coup launched by a faction of the military on 15 July has resulted in a massive purge by the Erdoğan government.**

Reckless military adventurism has weakened, possibly fatally, what was left of Turkey's democratic framework. In addition, it left more than 200 dead and over 1,500 injured, mostly civilians who went onto the streets to resist the coup.

The extent of the witch-hunt is staggering: 100 generals arrested—that's one third of the total; 6,000 military personnel arrested; 9,000 police sacked; 3,000 judges suspended, while this afternoon (19 July) the BBC reported that over 15,000 education staff had been suspended and the resignation of more than 1,500 university deans had also been ordered by Turkey's higher education (YÖK) board.

The board accused the staff of having links to Fethullah Gülen, a US-based Islamic cleric and one-time Erdoğan supporter, who the Turkish government says was behind Friday's uprising. The licences of 21,000 teachers working in private institutions have also been revoked.

President Erdoğan was quick to lay the blame on Gülen for the attempted coup, and his acolytes have taken up the hue and cry across civic society. Mr Gülen denies the charge and has condemned the attempted coup.

Journalists also suffered: at least one has paid with his life. According to the European Federation of Journalists (EFJ), Mustafa Cambaz, photo-journalist for the Turkish daily Yeni Şafak was killed by soldiers on Friday night in the Çengelköy neighbourhood of Istanbul during the attempted coup.

Soldiers also took control for a while of the state broadcaster TRT (the Turkish Radio and Television Corporation), the private broadcasters CNN, Turk and Kanal D, and the daily newspaper Hürriyet.

In the Ankara studios of TRT, news anchor Tijen Karaş was forced by coup soldiers to read a statement at gunpoint and several journalists were attacked during the clashes.

The EFJ also reported that, in Istanbul, civilians protesting the coup beat Selçuk Şamiloğlu, a photojournalist for Hürriyet and the

*Second time around*

Associated Press and, today, Turkey's media regulatory body revoked the licences of 24 radio and TV channels which they accused of having links to the Gülen movement. This gave the state virtual control of all but a few media outlets. Erdoğan was also quick to respond to demands for the reintroduction of the death penalty, which was abolished in 2004 as part of Turkey's bid to join the EU—by refusing to rule it out. In response, the EU said that if it were to be reintroduced it would end accession talks between the parties. That does not seem to bother Erdoğan at the moment. After all, he will be calculating that his chances of winning a referendum on his demands to become a president with executive powers look a lot better than they did a week ago.

Meanwhile in another twist in the story, today's Hürriyet Daily News reports that the army first received intelligence that a coup was under way on Friday, some hours before soldiers deployed tanks and targeted key infrastructure. According to the BBC, 'The General Staff said in a statement it alerted the relevant authorities, adding that the majority of members had nothing to do with the coup.'

Just who knew what and when is still unclear, but certainly the present beneficiary of all this is President Erdoğan.

### Update

*At the end of November 2020, a Turkish court sentenced leaders of the attempted coup to life imprisonment, convicting 337 former army officers, pilots and other suspects for life over the failed effort to overthrow the Erdoğan government. Seventy people were acquitted.*

*Estimates at the time of the attempted coup reported that more than 250 people were killed when a faction of the military seized warplanes, helicopters and tanks to take control of institutions and overthrow the government. They were directed from an airbase near Ankara.*

*The trial of over 400 defendants was the highest profile of dozens of court cases targeting thousands of people accused of involvement in the attempted coup.*

## 18  More trials pile up

### 25 September 2016

Last week I was on a mission to Turkey on behalf of the International and European Federations of Journalists (IFJ/EFJ) to observe a number of trials of journalists.

These have been on the increase since the failed coup of 15 July and the three-month state of emergency introduced on 21 July.

Under the state of emergency, some 131 media organisations, including three news agencies, 16 television channels, 23 radio stations, 45 daily newspapers, 15 magazines and 29 publishing houses have been closed (according to Early Day Motion 474 tabled in the UK parliament on 15 September). The Turkish authorities can also hold suspects in detention without charge for 30 days, with journalists frequently detained.

So it was against this background that together with the EFJ's project officer Mehmet Köksal we made our way to the Çağlayan Justice Palace in Istanbul on Tuesday, 20 September.

The first hearing was against journalists Ayse Düzkan, Ragip Duran, Hüseyin Akyol and Inan Kizilkaya.

The four are being prosecuted for participating in a solidarity campaign with the Kurdish daily newspaper Özgür Gündem. During the hearing, in a tightly controlled court room, the defendants complained that following the raid by heavily armed special police on 16 August, the offices of Özgür Gündem had been shut down, leaving the defendants unable to get into the building, or to collect their files or belongings.

One spoke of being kept in isolation with very limited access to lawyers, family and friends.

Inan Kizilkaya concluded: 'We didn't get any document from the prosecution, nor could we properly prepare my defence. All our work is related to journalism and freedom of expression and I don't consider it a criminal activity.'

After a 20-minute hearing, the judges decided to merge the case with 20 other similar ones and to resume on 15 December 2016.

We had only just got into the court in time to hear the case. A small room had been chosen which only seated some 40 observers. On leaving the court the defendants were greeted by dozens of supporters in the corridor who had been unable to get into the court.

Before the case started, supporters gathered outside the courthouse to make public statements of solidarity and we were joined by representatives from DISK Basin-İş Sendikası (Journalists Union of Turkey, part of DISK—the Confederation of Progressive Trade Unions of Turkey), TGS members (Journalists Union of Turkey), TGC (Turkish Journalists' Association), Kurdish journalists, members of Turkish Parliament, other members from the confederation, feminist activists, and friends.

It was an impressive turnout, leaving me in no doubt that, despite the post-coup increase in repression and atmosphere of fear, people were prepared to stand up for journalism and freedom of expression.

Asked by a local reporter why I was there, I replied: 'Every trial against a journalist is important, and we are here to express the solidarity of the international community for all our colleagues who are on trial for only doing their jobs. The situation is worse now than before 15 July because of the massive purges undertaken by the authorities. But the level of support shown this morning to the defendants shows the strong spirit of those defending press freedom and the public's right to information.'

Afterwards we made a solidarity visit to Evrensel newspaper. This left-wing Turkish daily newspaper has recently been under heavy media attacks from pro-governmental news organisations and from the government.

Fatih Polat, the Editor-in-Chief, gave examples of different types of threats they had received, including the jailing of correspondents in Mardin and Diyarbakir (south-east Turkey), pressure on advertisers, and penalties from the regulators. He explained the importance of international solidarity to put pressure on the authorities.

He specifically thanked the IFJ/EFJ and other media organisations for sending letters to Turkish authorities which helped secure the release of two Evrensel correspondents who had been taken into custody for over 15 days.

That evening, together with Ugur Güç, TGS president, I was interviewed on an evening news programme on IMC TV. We discussed the increasing number of prosecutions against journalists.

Responding to a question from presenter Banu Güven, I explained that, 'One of our strategies is to put pressure on European decision-makers to speak out against press freedom violations in Turkey and make them more active on this issue.'

I added that the IFJ/EFJ will continue its solidarity campaign, working with our affiliates in Turkey to improve the situation, in order to guarantee the public's right to information as well as mobilising our international affiliated unions around the world.

*You can view the programme at:*

*http://www.imctv.com.tr/efj-turkiye-gozlemcisi-gazetecilerle-dayanismaya-devam-edecegiz/*

When we left the studio, the thunderstorms and heavy rain had cleared, but there are more stormy times ahead. The next day (Wednesday, 21 September) we again arrived at the Çağlayan Justice Palace, which was hearing five different prosecution cases against journalists that day. We had originally been told that there would only be one.

Again, we were with the IFJ/EFJ affiliates TGS, DISK Basin-İş and TGC to observe the following cases:

1. The appeal in the MIT Trucks case, where journalists Can Dündar and Erdem Gül working for Cumhuriyet newspaper had been sentenced to five years in jail for revealing state secrets and arms trafficking between Turkish intelligence services (MIT) and Syrian armed rebel groups. The appeal hearing was held in secret, but this did not put off the many supporters, including Can's wife, who turned up to the court. Can was not present as he is currently living in Germany. (He has said that he will not consider returning until after the state of emergency has been lifted.) A further hearing has been ordered.

The next trial (which we could attend) was the long running Odatv case (see 1 'Four journalists freed in Turkey'; 5 'Odatv trials—more of the same'; 6 'The trials grind on'; 11 'OdaTV trial—more delays; talks start on forming a coalition government').

Here, investigative journalists were accused of being members of a secret illegal organisation called Ergenekon, which was trying to topple the government. The trial has been running for six years, despite the overwhelming evidence of the journalists' innocence and the fact that previous prosecutors and judges are either in jail or have fled the country for allegedly being themselves members or supporters of an illegal terrorist organisation (the Gülen movement, see (again) 1, 'Four journalists freed in Turkey' and 17, 'Botched coup gives Erdoğan the green light for massive purges'). The new judge refused to drop the charges in the absence of a newly appointed prosecutor and adjourned the case to 24 October.

During an exchange with one of the defendants, who asked for justice and that President Erdoğan (when he was Prime Minister) be named as one of the main supporters of Gülenists and therefore a co-accomplice in the plot against the internet TV station, eyebrows were raised when the judge replied: 'What justice? What fair trial are you looking for? Obviously there is nothing like that in this country

*Second time around*

anymore. You are journalists, no? You should be more aware of the situation than the rest of us, no?'

After being further pressed by a lawyer for one of the defendants, the judge agreed that the name be mentioned in the judicial record. Just whether the same judge will be presiding at the next hearing on 24 October remains to be seen.

Other cases were a follow-up on Özgür Gündem solidarity case (heard yesterday 20 September) where a journalist was asked to testify in another court; journalist Hasan Cemal being accused of insulting the Turkish president; and journalists and writers Mehmet Altan and Ahmet Altan, brothers who are still held in custody for allegedly giving 'subliminal messages suggesting a military coup' during a TV show.

Post-coup, the Turkish authorities have promoted the country to being the world leader for locking up journalists, while the state shuts down media outlets that don't toe the government line.

The need for international solidarity has never been greater and the IFJ/EFJ's continuing work, assisted by a new project funding from the European Union is crucial.

So is the need for journalists in Turkey to stand together, to defend the right to report and the public's right to information. This is not easy to achieve, but the mood of our IFJ/EFJ affiliates in Turkey is determined and positive.

## 19  The silencing of the media

### *10 November 2016*

**In 18, 'More trials pile up', I described the interview I gave with Ugur Güç, TGS (Journalists Union of Turkey) president, on an evening news programme on the television channel, IMC TV.**

We discussed the increasing number of prosecutions of journalists and, during the interview, presenter Banu Güven, explained that their television station had been threatened with closure.

Within two weeks they had indeed been taken off air, their equipment seized and the journalists and other media and support workers had joined the growing numbers of unemployed (reported on the EFJ website on 24 October at 2,500).

Recently I received an eyewitness (necessarily anonymous) account, reproduced below, of the events leading up to the closure of IMC TV.

On 4 October, members from RTÜK (Higher Board for Radio and Television) came to IMC TV accompanied by a dozen policemen and a couple of officials from the Ministry of Finance. It had already been four days since we were informed about our fate by a pro-government/pro-Erdoğan newspaper's website. Although we could not confirm the news, because no one from RTÜK had any information, and the Vice Premier in charge (Mr Numan Kurtulmuş) did not return our calls, we anticipated that they would soon appear at our door.

It was around noon when this group arrived in our studios. We were broadcasting live from the studio. One of my colleagues was interviewing the coordinator of the channel, Eyüp Burç, about the media crackdown by Erdoğan. Another team of the same composition had just raided the offices of Hayatın Sesi TV. We were expecting them any moment.

The first thing they wanted was to go to the control room, but to do that they had to cross the studio, passing before the cameras. They wanted to avoid showing themselves and their faces to the public. But we gave them no other option. They rushed across the studio.

Once they were in the control room, they asked our technicians to shut down the equipment and to cut off the signal. At this moment, there were two live pictures on the screen. One from the control room showing what was going on there, the other from the studio filled with IMC employees. While the RTÜK officials, along with the police, were ordering to shut down the machines one after the other, we were chanting slogans like 'Free press cannot be silenced!'

It was an emotional moment, some of my colleagues couldn't stop their tears. We were still on air but knowing that soon our signal would go off, we also used Periscope to keep on going live on social media, as IMC TV and also individually, we were live on Periscope, too.

I also entered the control room and there I asked: 'What are you planning to do here?'

The guy answered: '"We are planning to fulfil the orders.'

These orders were given by the Vice Prime Minister, who had been apparently warned about our 'activities', endangering national security, by a three-member committee.

A masterpiece of Erdoğan's state of emergency.

After our signal disappeared we moved on with Periscope. However, the police were uncomfortable with the many smart phones capturing these moments live. Once again, they were afraid showing their faces. The police chief warned me as I was on air on my phone. I responded saying that he should please back off. He did.

In the control room, there was this discussion: if they could confiscate the equipment there, and to what extent they would seal our working space. They had to discuss the issue of confiscation because we had rented all the equipment in the control room. As for the issue of sealing the offices, our CEO convinced them not to seal the main entrance. Only the control room was sealed at the end. The equipment there was registered by the state TV, TRT as trustee.

We had many visitors, colleagues who came for support. Solidarity made us feel good, however one major problem persists: unemployment. Since then, around 120 journalists and employees only at IMC TV are jobless with no or little possibility to find themselves work in this media landscape.

Since then the crackdown against dissenting voices has been stepped up.

On 30 October, the EFJ reported that the Turkish government issued a decree shutting down 15 Kurdish media outlets: 11 newspapers, two news agencies and three magazines. The latest closures brought the number of media outlets shut down under state of emergency to 168. Subsequently, a number of leading MPs from the Kurdish HDP (Peoples' Democratic Party) were arrested and subsequently jailed. The government then acted swiftly to block access to social media to shut down protests.

At the same time Turkish police detained the editor and at least 12 senior staff of Turkey's secular Cumhuriyet newspaper—one of the country's oldest newspapers. The editor-in-chief, Murat Sabuncu, the cartoonist, Musa Kart, the paper's lawyer and several columnists were detained, some following raids at their homes. According to the paper, police also had warrants for the detention of 16 staff members.

On 5 November the EFJ website reported that the Turkish court had sentenced nine executives and columnists of Cumhuriyet newspaper to prison.

In response, Johannes Hahn, EU Commissioner for European Neighbourhood Policy, issued a statement saying that: 'The scale of detentions, dismissals and shut-downs, notably in the media sector, based on charges of alleged terrorism, is highly questionable.'

*More at: http://europeanjournalists.org/blog/2016/10/24/turkey-107-journalists-in-prison-and-2500-others-left-unemployed/*
*http://europeanjournalists.org/blog/2016/10/31/new-wave-of-repression-targeting-daily-cumhuriyet-in-turkey/*

# 20 Turkey's democracy is being frozen out
## 21 January 2017

The weekend the SPOT (Solidarity with the People of Turkey) delegation arrived in Istanbul, the city was in the grip of freezing temperatures and the heaviest snowfalls for 20 years with over 65cm of snow paralysing the city.

When we arrived, a few days later, on 11 January, much of the snow and ice had thawed, but it was obvious that the country's democracy was still in the grip of a deep freeze and the temperature was plunging.

Our visit to the Turkish Journalists Association (TGC) set the scene. They told us that last year the authorities revoked the press cards of 780 journalists (making it next to impossible for them to do their work). Eight hundred and thirty-nine journalists were dragged before the courts because of the news they had recorded—a common charge is that they had been spreading terrorist propaganda.

A total of 189 journalists were subject to physical and verbal abuse and 144 journalists spent the New Year behind bars.

The number of unemployed journalists exceeds 10,000, many of them experiencing extreme financial hardship, as the state often makes it difficult for them to access unemployment benefits. Those opposition newspapers that are still publishing struggle against this background, with additional problems with distribution and finance—the result of pressure on advertisers to stop using the papers.

The Association also highlighted difficulties in promoting solidarity with all journalists, especially with those working for government-supporting media—some of which have called for the Association to be shut down and have been attacking critical journalists for being associated with the Kurdish/left party PKK or the Gülenist movement (accused of being behind the failed 15 July coup—see page 31, 'Botched coup gives Erdoğan the green light for massive purges'.)

Despite overwhelming odds ('We have never suffered such difficult times,' the union said), it remains determined to fight back against censorship and increasing attacks on free journalism.

During our visit to the Journalists Union of Turkey (TGS), in addition to hearing about journalists out of work, we heard of many held for four months without any court appearances (detention without trial); 170 media outlets closed down and journalists facing not only job insecurity but personal insecurity. They stressed the importance of international solidarity and the need to keep world attention focused on what is happening to the media in Turkey, which strengthened their work in campaigning for the release of those in prison for just doing their jobs.

President Erdoğan's Justice and Development Party (AKP) rules under a state of emergency introduced days after the failed 15 July coup. It has resulted in a crackdown on basic human rights—120,000 people have lost their jobs, some 90,000 have been detained and more than 40,000 arrested. Those journalists in detention are not allowed access to books and newspapers. Family visits are restricted to every 15 days, and lawyers' visits are extremely limited, with all interviews recorded by the authorities.

The impact of the emergency powers and the threat of a new constitution, which will also give absolute powers to President Erdoğan, were raised in our discussions with representatives of the newspapers we visited: Evrensel, Ozgurlukcu Demokrasi, Cumhuriyet and BirGün (and later when we visited opposition parties). All made a lasting impression, but perhaps the greatest was at the opposition paper Cumhuriyet, under constant threats from the government, which wants to close it down.

I was shocked to see that Cumhuriyet operates from a fortified office, (not far from Trump Towers) with an armed guard posted at the entrance, to prevent a Charlie Hebdo style attack. The paper is facing serious financial difficulties, without any income from advertising (the result of government pressure). But even with a greatly reduced staff (many are in detention) they still sell some 50,000 copies daily, with some 1.4 million hits on their website. Their readers are their greatest asset and are encouraged to build the paper's circulation and give financial support.

Our visits to opposition parties gave us the opportunity to question them about their strategies for campaigning against the new constitution (approved by Parliament), which is scheduled to go to a referendum in the spring. The CHP (Republican Peoples' Party) MP we met talked about the way they intended to mobilise neighbourhoods in Istanbul. The EMEP (Labour Party) representatives painted a vivid picture of the impact of the state of emergency, which not only banned strikes and marches, but threatened the abilities of opposition groups to organise.

They intended to work with other parties in a 'Say No' campaign, which would also link into opposition to the emergency powers in force post-coup. They also highlighted increasing economic difficulties hitting working people and their families. The response from Erdoğan has been to blame foreign governments of planning to bring down the economy and the government and to call on people to sell their dollars!

During our visit to the HDP (Peoples' Democratic Party a Kurdish/Turkish socialist party) we learned first-hand of the arrests of 12 of their MPs and co-chairs on 4 November 2016. One MP, Leyla Birlik, MP for Sirnak (a Kurdish town in south-east Turkey), was released from prison on 4 January but, at the same time, there were further arrests of leading members in Istanbul and their offices were raided.

They told us that, just days before we arrived, the government issued three decrees, expelling 8,398 more public employees, and 649 academics (30 of them had signed the Petition for Peace). Even government sources admit that, as at 10 January, the number of expelled state employees reached 135,000. Eighty-three more civil society organisations had been banned, bringing the total to over 1,400. These included the Istanbul Kurdish Institute founded in 1992, and a number of women's and lawyers' organisations. We also received details of 74 imprisoned co-mayors from the Kurdish regions, and their replacement by government 'Trustees'.

All those we met painted a grim picture, but were strong and determined to win out on what to us seem overwhelming odds. All emphasised the importance of international solidarity, which we were assured does make a difference. It is also important that we step up the political pressure on our MPs and government as well as on the European institutions, including the Commission and the Parliament.

But most of all it's about getting the message out to people through the press and our organisations, trade unions and civil society, telling them what's going on in Turkey, how the Kurdish communities are under attack with much of south-east Turkey under military control and what we can do about it.

Our solidarity is vital.

## 21  Odatv trial—after six years, is acquittal likely on 15 February?

*10 February 2017*

**Next Tuesday, I will be travelling to Istanbul to see the curtain come down on one of the most farcical trials of journalists I have witnessed in my years as an observer of such events in Turkey.**

The case began in 2011, when journalists and others on the internet news station, Odatv, were accused of being involved in a plot to overthrow the government and being part of the 'Ergenekon Terrorist Organisation'. Among those charged was journalist Muyesser Yildiz (who was adopted by the NUJ some five years ago), and I have covered the trial in my blogs since that time (the last report was on 25 September 2016—see 18 'More trials pile up').

According to a report in the Hürriyet Daily News after a hearing in December:

> In the eighth hearing of the case, 13 suspects, which included writers and journalists Ahmet Şık, Yalçın Küçük, Nedim Şener and Hanefi Avcı, prosecutor Ali Kaya said there was insufficient evidence over the allegations made against the suspects, who were initially accused of being involved in activity that was beyond the remit of journalism.
>
> The prosecutor argued that there was insufficient evidence over the existence of the Ergenekon organization, which was dismissed by the Supreme Court of Appeals in April 2016. The court ruled that the 'Ergenekon Terrorist Organisation', the source of all the allegations, did not actually exist, and dropped all charges in the case that accused the organisation of being Turkey's deep state ...

So, along with dozens of other supporters, I will be in the Istanbul court on 15 February to see the end of a trial which should never have begun.

The Odatv journalists are likely to be acquitted, but there are some 150 journalists still in prison, and being victimised by the state for just doing their jobs as journalists.

Turkey remains the world's biggest prison for journalists.

There will be no letting up in our solidarity.

## 22 The end of a farcical trial? Odatv trial: justice still denied?

*26 February 2017*

**Two weeks ago, I wrote 'Next Tuesday I am travelling to Istanbul to see the curtain come down on one of the most farcical trials I have witnessed in my years as an observer at trials of journalists in Turkey.'**

Because of an unscheduled trip to hospital in London and subsequent operation, I never made it to Turkey and the judicial farce continued when the newly appointed judge refused to dismiss the Odatv case, as called for by the Istanbul prosecutor. (See page 42, 'Odatv trial—after 6 years, is acquittal likely on 15 February?')

Judging by reports I received, it seems that before the case opened over 250 journalists, friends and activists gathered outside the court in Istanbul on 15 February.

They were not allowed to enter the courtroom because it was 'too small'.

I was told that, 'After heated debates with the guards, three people were permitted to enter the courtroom to hear the legal submissions. Meanwhile, outside supporters chanted: "Ahmet will get out [of jail] and will resume writing"—referring to the arrested journalist Ahmet Şık, one of the Odatv journalists on trial. The group gathered later in front of the courthouse with a big banner saying: "The plot is ongoing. We haven't remained silent and we won't."'

After six years of court hearings and the prosecutor now seeking the release of all the suspects, the judge decided to resume hearing the case on 12 April.

Whether he will bring the curtain down on this Alice in Wonderland trial remains to be seen.

## 23 At last, the Odatv 13 are acquitted
### 12 April 2017

**After a six-year ordeal, on 12 April an Istanbul court ordered the acquittal of 13 'suspects', including journalists and writers, charged with membership of the Ergenekon organisation (a group accused of plotting to overthrow the government).**

This was the final part of the long-running Odatv case. Among those acquitted is journalist Muysser Yildiz, who was adopted in a solidarity move by the NUJ in 2012.

According to press reports, the court unanimously acquitted the suspects, including journalists Ahmet Şık, Nedim Şener, Soner Yalçın, Yalçın Küçük and former police chief Hanefi Avcı, based on their pleas, expert reports, witness statements and 'the wider context of the file'.

It is also reported that those acquitted have the right to file a claim for compensation within one year of the verdict being given. The court also ordered a legal complaint to be filed against those who created fake digital evidence and sent it to the computers of those charged, along with public officials who acted in cooperation against the defendants during the investigation process.

The case was initiated in 2011 after police raided the suspects' addresses, and came at a time when all the suspects had been making broadcasts and writing articles criticising the trials relating to the Ergenekon organisation. These saw the arrests of over 200 people in a decade-long legal battle over allegations that they were aiming to overthrow the Turkish government.

Those in the Ergenekon case were charged with membership of an illegal organisation, trying to create an environment of chaos, inciting people to hostility and hatred, obtaining and revealing secret documents, attempting to influence a fair trial, and illegally recording personal data.

From the start, the journalists were supported by the European Federation of Journalists (EFJ) and its affiliate in Turkey, the Turkish Journalists Union (TGS).

Over the past six years I have regularly attended their hearings in Istanbul as a representative of both the EFJ and the International Federation of Journalists (IFJ). Over the past five years I have made regular reports of these trials—some of which bordered on farce.

Following the acquittal ruling, journalist and writer Amhet Şık said the case should be a lesson for judicial authorities who prepared the recent indictment against Cumhuriyet (an opposition newspaper) columnists and executives.

'This (Odatv) case should be a lesson for those who wrote the Cumhuriyet indictment. Those judges and prosecutors will also come here. We will present a life that will make the dreams of our children come true,' he said.

Şık had been tried without arrest in the Odatv case, but he is currently in jail in a separate case, having been arrested on 30 December 2016 on charges of 'making propaganda' for the outlawed PKK and the Fethullahist Terrorist Organisation (FETÖ).

In addition, there are some 150 journalists still in prison who, like the Odatv media workers, are being victimised by the state for doing their jobs as journalists.

Turkey remains the world's biggest prison for journalists. There must be no letting up in our solidarity, no matter what the outcome of the 16 April referendum turns out to be. This proposes 18 amendments to the constitution, including establishing a presidential system of government and a weakening of parliamentary powers referendum.

## 24 UK report criticises Turkey's human rights record—but how will government react?

### 18 April 2017

'**The UK has distinguished itself as a friend in the eyes of the Turkish government, and both sides are seeking to cement a strategic relationship. But, as the UK does so, it must not be seen as disregarding—or even excusing — allegations of serious human rights violations and the erosion of democracy in Turkey. It is vital that the UK's criticism both privately and publicly is not withheld when grounds for criticism exist.**'

Thus runs an extract from the recent UK parliament's Foreign Affairs Committee report, *The UK's Relations with Turkey*, published 21 March following eight months of review and consideration of evidence submitted by interested parties, including the NUJ and the TUC.

The report articulates the dilemma of considering human rights versus business, trade and strategic and 'security' interests.

The government's record to date on this is not good (witness the current debate about UK relations with Saudi Arabia). Everything comes with a price tag. But at least the report recognises that the post-15 July 2016 purges undertaken by the Erdoğan regime and in the run up to the constitutional referendum on 16 April are serious enough to recommend that Turkey is listed as a Human Rights Priority country by the Foreign and Commonwealth Office. But will this bring about a change of behaviour by Erdoğan?

Chapters 4, 5 and 6 of the report cover the status of human rights in Turkey and 'examine significant concerns about the erosion of ... human rights and democracy in Turkey.'

The NUJ, which submitted written evidence to the committee, is extensively quoted on pages 58—60, in the section dealing with Freedom of Expression. It criticises the government's post-coup purges and subsequent emergency powers as going 'far beyond the circumstances of the coup ...', the number of people who have been punished as 'extraordinary and their means of redress inadequate.'

The wide-ranging report also criticises the attacks on the Kurdish communities and continuing detention of opposition MPs, and goes into considerable detail about the alleged role of the Gülenist movement and individuals in the coup. It criticises the Foreign and Commonwealth Office for being broadly willing to take the Turkish government's account of Gülenist involvement in the coup 'at face value and seemed unable to offer an independent analysis.' (The committee took evidence from [the Foreign and Commonwealth Office] including at an oral hearing.)

Yet, despite all this, the committee welcomed the £100 million arms deal and encouraged the expansion of bilateral trade between the two countries.

The report was critically received by SPOT (Solidarity with the People of Turkey), who called on the government to at least halt all arms deals with the Turkish state.

With the Commons into its Easter recess, it's not known when, or even if, the report will be debated, so now is the time to contact your MP calling on him or her to demand a parliamentary debate.

*You can read the report at:*
*https://www.publications.parliament.uk/pa/cm201617/cmselect/cmfaff/615/615.pdf?wpisrc=nl_todayworld&wpmm=1*

*The Gülenist response to the report dated 25 March may be found at: http://www.dialoguesociety.org/press-release/1125-guelenist-response-to-the-foreign-affairs-committees-report-on-turkey-and-uk-relations.html#.WOPNwmco_cc*

# 25 A divided country
## 21 April 2017

**Erdoğan's narrow victory in the recent constitutional referendum shows Turkey is bitterly split as international monitors strongly criticise the campaign.**

The margin will not please President Erdoğan, who was hoping for a decisive win. Instead, it was just by a whisker, with an estimated 51.4 per cent of the vote, despite controlling the media and conducting the 'Yes' campaign under a state of emergency (extended for a further three months on 17 April) which limited the ability of opponents to openly campaign for a 'No' vote and meant that essential fundamental campaigning freedoms were denied.

Despite saying that the vote was 'well administered', the Organisation for Security and Co-operation in Europe (OSCE) and the Council of Europe were critical of the campaign, saying that it was an 'unlevel playing field' and the two sides of the campaign 'did not have equal opportunities'.

'In general, the referendum did not live up to Council of Europe standards,' said Cezar Florin Preda, head of the Council of Europe delegation. The delegation's criticisms were quickly rejected by President Erdoğan, who did not accept their comments and demanded that they should 'know their place'.

But the report will give confidence to opposition parties, who have many criticisms about the way the referendum and the vote were conducted, to pursue their concerns about abuses.

When I last visited Istanbul in January (see 39, 'Turkey's Democracy Being Frozen Out') I was impressed by the determination of many in the 'Vote No' camp to get out and campaign amongst the people, despite the odds.

They did remarkably well to achieve the majority 'no' votes in Istanbul, Ankara and Izmir, the three biggest cities in Turkey. And within hours of the provisional result being announced, Morning Star journalist Steve Sweeney, who is in Turkey covering the referendum, was reporting on social media that opposition demonstrations were growing in many districts of Istanbul and other places, with the simple message that 'We will resist.'

'The pots and pans heard across Istanbul on Sunday night were a reminder of the spirit of Gezi Park,' he said.

There are reports that some journalists covering opposition demonstrations in various places have been arrested.

But make no mistake, the victory—no matter how narrow—is a vote for an increasingly authoritarian and autocratic regime. The rule of law, the Odatv judgement not withstanding, is becoming a distant memory, along with the separation of powers and memories of an independent and critical media. And it is significant that within hours of the result Erdoğan was calling for the reintroduction of the death penalty.

A longstanding colleague of mine in Turkey, a former journalist, now a lawyer, emailed shortly after the result was announced as follows:

> It was a shady referendum. Not only in terms of propaganda period but mainly in terms of the security of boxes. It seems that the powers prepared the ground for every kind of trick. From now on, Erdoğan is a dictator not only de facto but also de jure. It is not the rule of law but the rule of Erdoğan. For 15 years, we were asking ourselves if it could be possible to see worse than the current situation. Every time we saw the worse one. Journalist arrests, suicide bombs, coup attempt, state of emergency ... And the final result is the worse than the previous bad ones. We are ones like in a marsh. Up to now, there were some pipes to get us breath, such as a little bit free media, some politicians, a few judges ... They were giving us a hope to live. Now all those pipes to breathe will be cut off.

### 19 April 8.13 am

***Update from Morning Star journalist Steve Sweeney:*** *'As I head back to London I would like to thank Turkey for the unexpected extra day in the country and for the Business Class ticket. I am on the plane so will be brief and will write more on my return. For now I leave with this message: The people of Turkey said No!'*

## 26  Odatv update/Two journalists face extradition from Spain

*10 August 2017*

**I have recently received an email from a relative of NUJ-adopted journalist Müyesser Yildiz, one of the journalists charged, imprisoned, released and subsequently acquitted on 12 April (see 23 '*At last the Odatv 13 are acquitted*').**

The writer tells me that since the coup attempt in July 2016, Müysser has been working extensively on reporting the trials of the people who are alleged by the authorities to have been involved in the failed uprising.

She has found serious allegations of torture, misconduct and unfair treatment of all sorts yet, practically speaking, a free press no longer exists in Turkey.

Much to the writer's surprise, the Odatv case eventually did conclude in favour of those on trial, but the political, judicial and even social aftermath of the attempted coup prevents them from feeling relieved, even after their six-year struggle.

The ecosystem of justice Turkey is harsh. Because of the unclear circumstances surrounding the events of July 2016, innocent people are being indicted, prosecuted and tortured alongside those who may be guilty. Yet, many people in Turkey blindly support this unjust approach: ignorance is disguised as patriotism.

'Anyway,' the writer concludes, 'that is a tad too broad and a little too dark a topic to cover in an e-mail exchange.'

Meanwhile, according to the European Federation of Journalists, around 160 journalists remain behind bars in Turkey, while a number of journalists living outside the country face arrest, imprisonment and trial if they return.

One is Hamza Yalçın, a Swedish-Turkish journalist who was arrested in Barcelona recently, following an international warrant issued by Turkey through Interpol, over alleged terrorist plots.

The European and International Federations of Journalists (EFJ/IFJ) together with their affiliates in Spain and in Sweden have strongly condemned the arrest and have urged the Spanish authorities not to hand Hamza Yalçın over to the Turkish authorities, as his safety, and the judicial independence of a trial, would not be guaranteed in Turkey.

A petition has been launched calling for his release.

In a new development, according to the BBC News website,

*Second time around*

German-Turkish writer Dogan Akhanli, author and a critic of the Turkish government, who was arrested in Spain at Turkey's request, has been granted conditional release by the Spanish authorities.

Dogan, who usually lives in Germany, where his arrest is seen as politically motivated, was on holiday in Spain when he was arrested.

According to his lawyer, Doğan Akhanli is being released on condition that he stays in Madrid.

**Further update at:**
https://www.geo.tv/latest/155995-erdogan-critic-urges-spain-to-block-his-extradition-to-turkey

## 27  Some good and some bad news
### 6 October 2017

**Hamza Yalçin (see 26, 'Odatv update/Two journalists face extradition from Spain') was released on 28 September following a decision by Spain's National High Court.**

'We are very pleased for our colleague, whose release we have been requesting since 3 August,' said European Federation of Journalists General Secretary Ricardo Gutiérrez. 'The Spanish Government has now to clarify that there is no basis to extradite Hamza Yalçin. There was simply no reason to arrest him: Interpol did not require his arrest.'

The decision was also welcomed by Margot Wallström, Swedish Minister for Foreign Affairs, who said: 'I welcome the Spanish decision not to hand out Hamza Yalçin to Turkey. Hamza Yalçin is now free to travel and can return to his family. Sweden has been working intensively with the case since the detention process became known and we have been clear that urgent and legal certainty has been necessary. All other questions are referred to the Spanish authorities'.

Meanwhile, according to Reporters Without Borders (RSF), a prosecutor in Diyarbakır in south-eastern Turkey, has asked the country's justice minister to obtain an Interpol 'red notice request' for the arrest of Can Dündar, a Turkish journalist and former editor of the Turkish daily, Cumhuriyet, now in exile in Germany, on a charge of propaganda for the outlawed Kurdistan Workers' Party (PKK).

In response, RSF has reiterated its call for an urgent overhaul of

Interpol because of the growing tendency for it to be exploited by repressive governments such as Turkey's.

The 'red notice request' came just one day after Can Dündar was nominated for the Nobel Peace Prize. He decided to stay in Germany in 2016 after being prosecuted on charges of 'divulging state secrets for espionage purposes' and 'assisting a terrorist organisation'.

According to RSF, the new PKK propaganda charge is based on a speech Dündar gave in Diyarbakır on 24 April 2016, in which he criticised the harassment of critical journalists and accused pro-government journalists of being accomplices to war crimes by supporting the government's military operations in Turkey's Kurdish provinces.

The grounds given by the Diyarbakır prosecutor's office for seeking the Interpol red notice was its inability to question Dündar in connection with this charge.

Julie Ward, Labour MEP for the North West of England, has already taken up the case.

After spending nearly 100 days in detention in late 2015 and early 2016, Dündar was sentenced to five years and ten months in prison in May 2016 (along with fellow Cumhuriyet journalist Erdem Gül) on the charge of 'divulging state secrets'. The court let him remain free pending the outcome of his appeal, but he was the target of a murder attempt as he left the courthouse in Istanbul.

The July 2016 coup attempt triggered an unprecedented purge against critical media outlets. In his farewell editorial in Cumhuriyet in August 2016 Dündar wrote that he would not return to Turkey, as the draconian emergency powers assumed by President Recep Tayyip Erdoğan since the coup meant he would not get a fair hearing.

'From now on, what we face would not be the court but the government,' Dündar said. 'To trust such a judiciary would be like putting one's head under the guillotine.'

He and Gül are still also being prosecuted on a charge of collaborating and supporting 'the FETÖ terrorist organisation' (the Gülen Movement) (see: 18 'More trials pile up').

The last hearing in the case was scheduled to be held on 4 October.

## 28 Turkish courts refuse order to release two journalists

### 15 January 2018

**Last Thursday, the Constitutional Court ruled that the pretrial detention of Mehmet Altan and Sahin Alpay violated their right to freedom of expression and said they should be released from Silivri prison.**

But, hours later, two separate Istanbul penal courts said they could not implement the decision because they had not been notified of the ruling.

Their decision was supported by Bekir Bozdaz, Turkey's Deputy Prime Minister, who criticised the constitutional court, accusing it of overstepping 'the limit set out in the constitution and the laws'.

Thursday's ruling had given hope to press freedom campaigners in Turkey, who are calling for the release of some 150 jailed journalists.

Alpay, a columnist for the now defunct newspaper Zaman, was arrested two weeks after the attempted coup of July 2016. Altan, an economist and writer, was arrested in September 2016 along with his brother, a former editor-in-chief of the newspaper Taraf, which was shut down after the attempted coup. Both have been accused of having 'links to terrorist groups' and 'attempting to overthrow the government'—charges they have denied.

PEN International, ARTICLE 19, the European Centre for Press and Media Freedom (ECPMF), the European Federation of Journalists (EFJ), Human Rights Watch (HRW), Index on Censorship, the International Press Institute (IPI) and Reporters Without Borders (RSF) have all campaigned on Altan's and Alpay's cases since their detentions, and submitted third party interventions on the cases to the European Court of Human Rights. They have all expressed dismay that the Constitutional Court's decision has not been carried out—and at the implications this has for the rule of law in Turkey.

Source: *Financial Times 13/14 January and EFJ website*

# 29 Conference calls for solidarity in action to help end repression in Turkey

*22 January 2018*

**As some 200 people assembled in London on Saturday, 20 January at the conference organised by Solidarity with the People of Turkey (SPOT), Turkish war planes launched air strikes on Afrin, one of the three Kurdish cantons in northern Syria.**

The conference coincided with the launch of a military operation with the support of the Free Syrian Army and cynically named operation 'Olive Branch'. Held at the headquarters of the National Education Union, it included workshops and panels made up of participants from Turkey and Britain. The morning session workshops featured women's resistance against the background of declining women's human rights and gender inequality, solidarity with academics, teachers and scholars at risk and political representation and the role of the UK parliament.

Speakers at the political workshop drew attention to the attacks on opposition members of the Turkish parliament (especially members of the pro-Kurdish party the HDP) which have been stepped up since the failed coup of July 2016, the removal and detention of many elected mayors in the Kurdish and south-eastern region of Turkey and their replacement by unelected administrators. Local administrations run by the main opposition party the CHP have also been targeted.

Panel member and Tottenham MP David Lammy, whose constituency has a high number of Kurdish residents, condemned the British government's sale of arms and aircraft to Turkey.

According to a Guardian report (22 January 2017):

…between 1 July and 30 September 2016, the UK sold Turkey £26m-worth of ML13 licences, which relate to exports of armoured plate, body armour and helmets. In addition, Britain sold Turkey £8.5m-worth of ML10 licences for aircraft, helicopters and drones, and almost £4m-worth of ML4 licences for missiles, bombs and 'counter-measures'.

> Since 2015 the UK has sold Turkey £330m-worth of arms. The country is on the Department for International Trade's list of 'priority markets' for arms exports…

Lammy said that, in the light of the July 2016 crackdown and state of emergency, pressure must be put on the UK government and that he and colleagues were intending to call for another parliamentary debate on the matter.

Workshops in the afternoon session covered attacks on workers and trades unions, what next for Turkey in the Middle East and the Kurdish question and journalism and the role of the media. Turkey is the biggest jailer of journalists in the world with some 150 journalists in prison and speakers with personal experiences outlined the extent of the crackdown on media and social media which had been stepped up since the failed July 2016 coup.

Speaking in the session, I outlined the solidarity work done by the International and European Federations of Journalists (IFJ and EFJ), along with my personal experiences of observing trials of journalists and visits to newsrooms, where journalists were often under threats of closure and violence.

Perhaps the most disturbing thing I learned was of personal threats to journalists and others living in exile. At least one well-known such journalist, now in Germany, faced death threats and was under constant guard, while in the same country it was reported earlier this month that Kurdish footballer Deniz Naki was in fear for his life after being shot at while driving along a motorway.

He had left Turkey after being subject to a racist attack in Ankara for expressing support for the Kurds.

Leaked intelligence reports have revealed possible assassination attempts on high-profile Turkish and Kurdish opposition figures such as academics and journalists living in Europe, especially Germany, who have spoken out against the Turkish government.

Everyone left the conference united in their determination to step up solidarity action and widen future campaigns with a call for unity in action to bring about the restoration of human and trade union rights, democracy and peace in Turkey—and see an end to the seemingly never-ending state of emergency which threatens the very fabric of society by paving the way for authoritarianism and dictatorship.

## 30  NUJ condemns journalists' jailings; judge rejects extradition demands

*15 December 2018*

**In an act of solidarity, the NUJ has decided to adopt jailed journalist Ayşe Düzkan.**

Ayşe, is a member of the board of DISK-Is, one of the NUJ's sister unions in Turkey and she has been defending herself for the last 18 months at various court hearings. Finally she was indicted earlier this month and was sentenced to 18 months in jail. The Istanbul court jailed her and other colleagues on charges of 'propagandising for a terrorist organisation'.  Hüseyin Aykol was also sentenced and given three years and nine months; Hüseyin Bektaş, Mehmet Ali Çelebi and Ragıp Duran were each given sentences of one year and six months in jail.

In a statement on the NUJ website, NUJ General Secretary, Michelle Stanistreet, said:

> News that leaders of our sister union DISK-Is have been sentenced is a massive blow to press freedom. The heavy sentences served on Ayse Düzkan and her four colleagues are a disgrace and a clear sign that the pressures facing journalists and journalism in Turkey show no sign of abating. Journalists are not terrorists and should be able to carry out their work without fear of intimidation and persecution. The world needs to make it clear to the Turkish regime that its brutal crackdown on journalists has to stop. Ayşe and all those other journalists currently in prison have the full support and solidarity of all NUJ colleagues throughout the UK and Ireland and we will do all we can to press for an end to their incarceration.

Meanwhile, on 28 November, the Guardian reported that a judge had thrown out an extradition request from the Turkish authorities for a media owner and three colleagues to be returned to Turkey to face trial in Ankara.

Akin Ipek's TV stations and newspapers have been confiscated by Turkish authorities for criticising the Erdoğan regime. The case was brought by the Crown Prosecution Services (CPS) on behalf of the Turkish government and heard at Westminster Crown Court in London at the end of November.

In the latest in a number of similar refusals by British courts, the request was dismissed as 'politically motivated' by Judge John Zani.

The judge also refused the request on the grounds that returning the four would put them at risk of serious mistreatment.

The case was the latest demanded by the Turkish government to return those alleged supporters of the Gülen movement who the authorities claim were involved in the July 2016 failed coup against the regime. The CPS has said that it will appeal the decision.

According to the NUJ, Turkey is the biggest jailer of journalists, with a record 180 in prison.

*NUJ website: https://www.nuj.org.uk/news/turkey-jails*

## 31  Turkey—democracy denied, but not yet lost

*14 February 2019*

**With democracy teetering on the edge and the country accelerating towards dictatorship under the autocratic rule of President Recep Tayyip Erdoğan, some 200 people attended last Saturday's third annual Solidarity with the People of Turkey (SPOT) conference in London.**

The purpose was to hear eyewitness reports from Turkey and the Kurdish community and to plan future solidarity action aimed at calling to account the Turkish government and to challenge the complicity of European governments in their support for the Erdoğan regime.

Opening the conference, Christine Blower (former General Secretary of the National Union of Teachers, and Vice Chair of Unite Against Fascism) reported on the current political situation.

The state of emergency introduced following the reckless and bloody July 2016 coup had been incorporated into law and an executive presidency had been firmly established, sidestepping parliament. She referred to the recent solidarity action by the NUJ in condemning the imprisonment of Ayşe Düzkan and four other journalists for just doing their jobs and to the solidarity message to the conference from the French journalist union SNJ-CGT. She also paid tribute to Labour Party leader Jeremy Corbyn for his message of support to the conference and long-standing solidarity with those resisting oppression in Turkey.

Jeremy's words of solidarity were echoed by Labour MP for Edmonton, north London, Kate Osamor, who also condemned the refusal of the British consulate in Istanbul to grant a visa to journalist and writer Dr Mehmet Arif Koşar, who was due to speak at the conference.

The NUJ had also protested to the consulate about the refusal. Kate Osamor went on to highlight the increasing oppression of women in Turkey. She declared that President Erdoğan was an enemy of women's rights whose policies encouraged their oppression. She pledged her continuing solidarity to the people of Turkey.

Writer Aydın Çubukçu reminded the conference that parliament had no powers and that the government saw the forthcoming local government elections in Turkey on 31 March as a vote of confidence. An opposition electoral alliance had been set up to fight these elections and he saw this as an important part of the fight back against dictatorship.

Speakers from the Republican People's Party (CHP) and the Peoples' Democratic Party (HDP) described the situation with the economy slowing down and greater media consolidation in the hands of the government, and over 90 per cent of the media being under its influence. There was also increasing violence against Kurds, women and minority groups. Reference was also made to growing inequality of wealth under the ruling Justice and Development Party (AFK) since 2002, while former HDP MP, Osman Baydemir, spoke about the increasing attacks on human rights in general and the Kurds in particular. He called for action to defeat fascism in Turkey, as in the past in Spain, Italy and Germany.

Two workshops followed the opening session, on the workers' fight back against ever-increasing attacks on their rights to organise; and on media censorship and criminalisation of journalists in a country that was the biggest jailer of journalists in the world.

Afternoon workshops considered how to preserve academic freedom in Turkey under authoritarian rule and democracy and the political landscape in Turkey. In the latter session Julie Ward MEP for North West England spoke of her visits to the region, the hostility she had faced from the authorities, the work she was doing in the European Parliament to raise awareness of the situation in Turkey and her efforts to put pressure on the European institutions to act in defence of civil and human rights.

The final plenary session debated what was being done in Turkey to fight for democracy and what we in the UK could do to continue to build solidarity, with speakers from the public services union UNISON, Stop the War Coalition, the Ethical Journalists Network and the Guardian Foundation.

*For more information about SPOT visit: www.spotturkey.co.uk*

## 32  NUJ member harassed and detained then deported by Turkish authorities for just doing his job

*31 March 2019*

**Today is municipal election day in Turkey when voters elect local mayors and councillors.**

President Recep Tayyip Erdoğan has said the poll is about the 'survival' of the country and his Justice and Development Party (AKP). Turkey is in recession, inflation is running at 20 per cent and the lira has plunged by a third in value, causing bankruptcies.

The result will be seen as a referendum on President Erdoğan's record and he knows it. One journalist who will not be covering the elections is NUJ member and Morning Star international editor Steve Sweeney.

Last week he flew out to Istanbul, but on arrival at the airport he was detained without explanation, questioned, branded a terrorist and deported. Steve takes up the story:

> My anticipated detention came shortly after my plane landed at Istanbul's Sabiha Gokcen airport—named after Kemal Ataturk's adopted daughter. She is famous for being Turkey's first female pilot. But what is glossed over is her role in using chemical bombs in attacks on Kurds during the massacre of Dersim in the 1930s.
>
> A police officer grabbed my phone out of my hand and bundled me into a holding area next to their office. The tiny smoke-filled room was already packed when I arrived. The 18 men looked puzzled and surprised at my arrival—I was the only person of non-Turkish or Middle Eastern appearance.
>
> Soon the numbers began to dwindle as one by one they started to let people go on their way. The longer I was there, the more serious I realised my situation was.
>
> I was photographed and forced to unlock my phone, making me nervous for the safety of others, despite taking stringent security measures prior to leaving London.
>
> But it made me feel violated and vulnerable. I am sure they have bugged my phone although I'm also sure that I have been monitored by Turkish security services for some time already.
>
> I was at no stage informed as to the reasons for my detention, nor was I told what was happening. I was unable to communicate with anybody to let them know what was happening and was not allowed to contact the British consulate, despite it being my legal right.

Unbeknown to me, friends on the outside had contacted the consulate and lawyers in Istanbul. But they too hit a brick wall as police denied that I was being held.

They were alerted when friends from the Peoples' Democratic Party (HDP) said I hadn't arrived on my plane to Diyarbakir. It was at this moment I was listed as a missing person.

The implications of this are sinister. With no record of my detention and a denial that I was being interrogated at the airport, anything could have happened to me. I could easily have disappeared at the hands of the Turkish state and they would simply have denied any knowledge of what had happened to me or my whereabouts.

The murder of Jamal Khashoggi flashed through my mind. It is not beyond the realms of possibility for the Turkish state to carry out a similar act.

My interrogation was brief and incompetent. After being asked some questions about what my intentions were in Diyarbakir, who I worked for and what my job was, they brought in a more senior officer to grill me further.

He opened by asking what I thought of Kurdish people. The subtext of his question was clear and gave an insight into the mindset of the Turkish state. I responded by saying that they were human beings, the same as everyone else and deserved to be treated as such.

He clearly didn't agree but my view of them marked me as a 'terrorist sympathiser' in his narrow nationalist mindset. The officer was trying his best to intimidate me, his eyes bulging as he raised the volume.

As he leaned across the table, he asked what I thought about the HDP. I responded that they were OK, a legal political party standing on a broadly social democratic platform—the Labour Party here has fraternal links, I explained.

This was circled as he scribbled on a scrap of paper—no official logbooks were used at any stage of the process. Later during the interrogation he asked me who Abdullah Öcalan was. I said most people know who he is and asked what he was getting at, knowing full well he was trying to link me to support for the Kurdistan Workers' Party (PKK).

He told me it was a terrorist organisation, banned in Turkey and proceeded to list its many crimes. The reality was he was trying to link the PKK with the HDP—exactly what Erdoğan has done in an attempt to rally opposition to the party and encourage violent attacks against it, often successfully.

The officer said MPs from the HDP had attended the funerals of suicide bombers and were instructing them to carry out attacks on Turkish citizens—none of which was backed by evidence.

More bizarrely he claimed that the HDP was instructed by Abdullah Öcalan—I questioned this as he has been jailed in isolation since 1999. However he claimed that Öcalan was sending messages to them through his lawyers.

When I explained that he had not seen his lawyers since 2011, he became angry—because he had been caught out. 'OK, you're probably right, but before then he definitely was,' he snapped.

"So Öcalan was giving instructions to the HDP before they even existed?' I asked, as, becoming irritated, he blasted that they were 'all terrorists,' the mask finally slipping.

By this stage I had been awake nearly 30 hours and was feeling exhausted and dizzy. Not only was I sleep-deprived but I had also been without food or drink for at least 12 hours, which was starting to affect me.

After another grilling by another team, I was finally on the move. No explanation was given as I was greeted by uniformed police. I was made to empty my pockets and sign two pieces of paper—I had no idea what they said and didn't think it made much difference, in all honesty.

This procedure was carried out by outsourcing giant ISS—mainly known in Britain for running hard and soft services in NHS hospitals and other public services extracting huge profits from the public purse.

I was then locked in a holding cell with around eight other men. Among their number included an Azeri, an Iraqi Kurd, three Turkmen, an Egyptian and two Saudi jihadists who seemed to want to kill me.

Finally I was called and told I was being sent back to London, again without being told why. I was escorted onto a Pegasus plane and boarded alone before the other passengers. I was still not allowed my phone or passport which were eventually handed to me by counter-terror police when I landed at Stansted airport in the early hours of this morning.

The paperwork said I was stopped from entering Turkey as I was deemed a national security threat—despite no evidence being offered as to the reasons for this decision. Turkish police had used Law No. 6458, the same that saw two members of the French Communist Party suffer a similar fate last week.

My visa was also cancelled and I was told that I would not be able to enter Turkey again without permission from the embassy—effectively banning me from the country.

Being banned from Turkey leaves me utterly heartbroken. I have many friends there who I will not see until there is a change in the brutal authoritarian government. And it is a country that, despite the dictatorial regime, has much to admire about it.

It is also a flagrant attack on press freedom and one which should not be taken lightly or accepted. I will be calling on the Foreign Office to take measures to ensure that journalists are able to report freely and without fear of arrest or intimidation.

Now is also the time for journalists and the labour movement to speak out against the atrocities and attacks on press freedom and democracy in Turkey. More journalists are in jail there than any other country in the world, with many others self-censoring for fear of reprisals.

Turkey is a difficult place for journalists and writers. A joke currently doing the rounds illustrates the gallows humour and sums up perfectly the seriousness of the situation. A prisoner goes to the jail's library to borrow a book. The librarian says: 'We don't have this book, but we have its author.'

Last month, through the NUJ London Central Branch, we agreed to launch a solidarity network for exiled journalists and those at risk—this is needed now more than ever so we will officially launch the organisation in the coming weeks.

The NUJ, trade unions and other organisations must throw their weight behind this initiative.

What has happened to me is a minor inconvenience. It does not compare to the thousands that have been arrested, jailed, tortured and killed under the yoke of Erdoğan's tyranny.

Many friends are included among those who are either banned from leaving Turkey or have been forced into exile, away from their families, friends and all that is familiar to them.

I have no doubt whatsoever that the decision to deport me and ban me from entering Turkey was a political one. HDP officials agree and warn it is a sign that the state is preparing huge violations during Sunday's local elections.

Erdoğan is fearful of the success of the HDP, which is bidding against all the odds to retake municipalities that have been stolen from the party. Nearly 100 mayors have been arrested and replaced by government-appointed trustees in the largely Kurdish areas.

Turkey's authoritarian president has already indicated he will do the same again, vowing to replace those with links to terrorist organisations should they win. There is no doubt he means the HDP which he insists is merely a front for the PKK.

But whatever happens on Sunday, elections are just a snapshot and what is important is what happens next. The opposition needs to adopt a strategic approach that goes beyond polls and prepares for the inevitable onslaught being prepared by the regime.

Erdoğan's is a mafia regime and it can only exist through its system of patronage and threats against political opponents and even its political allies.

Nobody is safe from the clutches of the tyrannical regime installed in Turkey. Süleyman Soylu—a former opponent of Erdoğan's and supporter of the shadowy Gülenist movement—struck a chilling tone last month when he called for holidaymakers to be arrested if they criticise the Turkish government.

But it is a regime that is propped up by Western imperialism which continues to support tyranny in Turkey. They have no interest in seeing a free and democratic Turkey. It would threaten imperialist interests in Syria, Iraq and Iran—all countries with vast oil reserves and all countries where they are pressing for regime change.

It is why they have remained silent over the human rights atrocities that are committed by Turkey both internally and in its wars and attacks on Kurds in Syria and Iraq.

Theresa May's appalling comments in a press conference last year—which I was blocked from attending—have serious consequences but also expose the attitude and agenda of the British government.

By praising Erdoğan for 'the fight against Kurdish terrorism', in one fell swoop she joined Erdoğan in branding an entire community as enemies of the state.

She has said in Parliament that she supports journalism, but what is the government doing to ensure that those reporting inside Turkey can do so safely and freely, without fear of arrest and intimidation?

Despite the threats and intimidation, I will not be silenced. I will continue to speak out about the crimes against freedom and democracy committed by the Turkish state. As a journalist it is my duty to shine a light in dark places.

This has made me more determined than ever to speak out and I will continue to write and challenge tyranny wherever it raises its head.

The best we can do in this country is to build a mass movement that brings down the Tory government and replaces it with one that has a foreign policy based on solidarity and co-operation, not war and profit.

*Note: Ataturk was the founder of modern Turkey after the collapse of the Ottoman Empire.*

*Steve Sweeney in the Morning Star Online, 29 March 2019: https://morningstaronline.co.uk/article/f/sweeney-banned-turkey*

## 33  Erdoğan faces his moment of truth by challenging the results

*11 April 2019*

**President Recep Tayyip Erdoğan called the local elections a matter of 'national survival'.**

His opponents were called terrorists and traitors. His grip on the media resulted in overwhelming positive coverage in the run-up to the election.

Yet although his ruling Justice and Development Party (AKP) nationally won just over 51 per of the votes on an 84 per cent turnout, the loss of major cities is a moment of truth for Turkey's authoritarian president.

Ankara, the capital, was won by the opposition secular Republican People's Party (CHP). Istanbul, Erdoğan's birthplace and former stronghold, is holding a recount he has demanded. So far the CHP maintains its narrow lead.

Below are the views of a well-placed source of mine in Ankara on the outcome of the election.

Q. Did the result come as a shock to you?
A. No. According to the poll results, it was foreseen that the big cities such as Izmir and Ankara would be won by the opposition coalition parties: the Good Party (İyi Parti) and the CHP who formed an electoral alliance. The Peoples' Democratic Party (HDP) did not field a candidate in Istanbul or Ankara, so HDP voters also supported the opposition coalition. So it was thought that AKP would lose Istanbul to the opposition. But of course it was a shock for AKP indeed.

Q. What role did the economy play in shifting support away from the AKP?
A. Economic crisis is the leading motive for the AKP supporters to change their votes.

Q. Erdoğan said that a victory in these elections was a 'matter of national survival'. What will be his reaction to the defeat?

A. Erdoğan clearly saw his defeat as the results came in on election night. It was difficult for him and his team to accept them and their first reaction was not to give up without a fight-back in Istanbul and the other places where they lost. This attitude indicates how they will behave in the next four years (until the next elections) and manage their relationship between the local authorities they lost and the governing regime. The AKP will not allow the municipalities won by opposition parties to act freely either economically or administratively.

Q. Will there be another crackdown (purge) to strengthen his position?
A. There are some indications that there is division within the AKP. As a reaction to the defeat, Erdoğan will make radical changes to the government and the administration of AKP. Erdoğan sees himself as not responsible for the defeat and seeks to shift the responsibility to people around him who will take the blame for the election results. They in turn are likely to resist taking the blame by using their power and influence over the bureaucracy and judiciary to avoid being purged.

Q. Will he use his presidential powers to replace some of the elected mayors? Will he take legal action to challenge the results that went against the AKP? What action do you think he will take against the Peoples' Democratic Party (HDP)? How will the Republican People's Party (CHP) build on these results?

A. Erdoğan has defined the new Istanbul CHP mayor as 'lame duck'. He also claims that the opposition parties have no majorities in the assemblies of the municipalities where the people elected CHP or HDP mayors and they can therefore not make any budgets or take major policy decisions. In effect it means that the opposition local mayors will be under the strict control of the President. HDP mayors will be accused of terrorist activities, while he hopes that CHP mayors will be restricted economically. There will be big political conflicts between the President and the opposition parties right up until the next general, presidential and local elections in 2023. There is also the possibility Erdoğan could call early elections if the political struggle increases and the economic crisis deepens.

Q. Do the results show that democracy is still alive despite the massive purges and crackdowns on the independent press?
A. If you accept democracy equals elections, you may say that democracy is alive in Turkey. But it's not the case. The governing AKP still has big control over media, judiciary, legislation (parliament), bureaucracy, military, police, intelligence, and all official institutions and private companies. As already mentioned, re-counting is taking place in the provinces where AKP lost and objections made by the opposition parties, especially by HDP, have been overruled.

After the elections in Istanbul, the police questioned members of the balloting committees (so-called ballot box committees) consisting of local political party representatives, public servants and the judges who head them up. This action was undertaken by the order of the public prosecution office. Members were questioned as to whether they have any relationship with so called 'terrorist organisations', especially Fethullah Gülen (FETO). This was an attempt to threaten and put pressure on members of the balloting committees, which are part of the national body that oversees the elections.

Under these conditions, we cannot say that democracy is alive in Turkey.

Q. Any other comments?
A. Before the elections, people believed that Erdoğan would apply every pressure to avoid losing. The developments after the elections show that he will use all powers of the state for private and political party interests and not for the public good. Before flying to Moscow shortly after the election, Erdoğan made a speech saying that challenges to the results will continue by judicial means if required.

On the other hand, the two main leaders of opposition coalition, Kemal Kılıçdaroğlu and Meral Akşener, held an important post election 'review' meeting. They are worried about Erdoğan's political influence over, and pressure he could put on, the Supreme Election Council (YSK), which oversees all elections in Turkey. It has the right to give the final ruling on the 31 March elections, including the Istanbul results. The AKP wanted all votes in Istanbul recounted, including 'invalid' votes (i.e. voting papers without the official mark or generally 'spoiled') but on 9 April their request was rejected by the YSK. The Istanbul result is very important for AKP because of the city's financial and economic significance.

Briefly, there is no democracy, there is no rule of law in Turkey. And yes, the results show that there is a partial reaction to the Erdoğan regime, but it is still the rule of Erdoğan in Turkey.

*This interview took place between 3 and 8 April.*

# 34 Election rerun forced in Istanbul as Turkey heads towards dictatorship and economic instability

## 12 May 2019

**Turkey's ruling party has reacted with fury at the loss of the Istanbul mayoral race to Ekrem İmamoğlu, from the opposition CHP (Republican People's Party) in the local elections on 31 March.**

President Recep Tayyip Erdoğan has secured a rerun of the election for Istanbul mayor to be held on 23 June. The party has refused to accept the result, claiming that there were 'irregularities and corruption' in the vote.

Under extreme pressure, Turkey's ruling electoral body, the higher election board (YSK) agreed, provoking anger in Turkey, especially in Istanbul and there are reports that there are concerns at the decision, which could have future political implications, even among some within the ruling Justice and Development Party (AKP). However, they did not order a rerun of votes for district administrators, mayors, and municipal councils in the city.

As soon as the decision was announced, the value of the Turkish lira fell to its weakest level in eight months, despite interventions to curb its decline. Meanwhile, the economy continues to decline, shrinking by 4 per cent in the first quarter of the year, according to an estimate by a research centre at Istanbul's Bahçeşehir University. The official figure is scheduled to be released in late May.

Another interesting aspect on the rerun decision was reported by Martin Chulov from Istanbul in the Guardian on 8 May. Under the heading 'Opposition claims rerun is to save Erdoğan's party finances', he reports that the losses of Izmir and Ankara were bad enough, but the Istanbul loss hit the hardest, 'posing threats to the

AKP's funding streams and organisational structure, which have long been sustained by the country's biggest city.'

Claims have been made that the previous AKP administrations made sure that large amounts of the budget given to the municipality were allocated to organisations tied to the Turkish government.

'For 25 years Istanbul has been a main source of income and financing their political movements,' says former MP and CHP member Barış Yarkadaş. 'According to the donation reports of the municipality this year 847m Turkish lira (£105m) was donated to foundations that are connected to the government; the Archery Foundation and another foundation for religious schools. They are like the back garden of AKP.'

There was also international condemnation of the decision to rerun the election. From the European Parliament, Guy Verhofstadt leader of the Alliance of Liberals and Democrats said that the decision was 'outrageous' and showed how Erdoğan's Turkey was drifting towards a dictatorship.

Whether these words, like those condemning Turkey's record on freedom of expression, will lead to any action by the EU is, of course, another matter.

# 35  Erdoğan loses rerun of Istanbul Mayor election

*24 June 2019*

**Voters in Istanbul have dealt a stunning blow to the prestige of President Erdoğan and a landmark victory for democracy.**

This came in the form of a landslide win for the opposition coalition candidate from the Republican People's party (CHP), Ekrem İmamoğlu, who for the second time was elected Mayor of Istanbul, over the former Prime Minister Binali Yıldırım, the candidate of the ruling Justice and Development party (AKP).

And what a victory it was.

Despite blanket pro-government media coverage, nearly 9 million people voted in the rerun election, representing some 85 per cent of those eligible to vote. In the March election, Ekrem İmamoğlu's majority was 13,500. This time is was some 775,000, representing just over 54 per cent of the votes cast. The decision to demand a rerun has been a disastrous one for Erdoğan and will have serious repercussions within the governing AK, which it was rumoured was split over the original decision to call for the rerun. After all, it was Erdoğan who said that 'whoever wins Istanbul will win Turkey'.

The vote is the biggest blow in his 25-year career to what seemed his dictatorial grip on power.

Writing in the Guardian (24 June), Bethan McKernan reported that:

> Losing Istanbul for a second time is an unthinkable outcome for the AKP. Turkey's biggest city and economic heart, it accounted for 31 per cent of GDP in 2017 and is an important driver of the government's unofficial patronage networks. It has been controlled by the ruling party and its Islamist predecessors for a quarter of a century.
>
> Observers note that İmamoğlu's mandate is still far from assured: the 2015 general election which saw the AKP lose its majority in parliament was rerun and other charismatic challengers to Erdoğan have been imprisoned or folded under pressure.
>
> The AKP still controls 25 of Istanbul's 39 districts and holds a majority in the municipal assembly, which will make it difficult for İmamoğlu to deliver on campaign promises. The margin of his victory, however, shows that at least in Istanbul there is a strong appetite for change after 16 years of national AKP rule.

This strong appetite for change was reflected in the measures some electors went to in order to cast their votes. The English language Hürriyet Daily News reported that:

> Fatma Tunca, a 77-year-old who recently had a hip surgery, was brought to a school in an ambulance in the Samandıra neighbourhood on the Asian side to cast her vote. She was one of the elderly and disabled people who were escorted by officials to the ballot boxes. The newly opened Istanbul airport also witnessed a busy day with thousands of people flocking to the districts where their addresses were registered. Long lines of buses were observed at the Esenler Bus Terminal on the European side of the city starting from 22 June.
>
> According to İbrahim Tansel from the Central Anatolian province of Sivas, the election offered an opportunity to see his friends while Dursun Çağlayan from the Black Sea province of Trabzon told Demirören News Agency at the airport that his family had businesses in both cities. 'We will cast our votes as a family and go back to Trabzon,' he said.

Ekrem İmamoğlu's campaign was supported by the Peoples' Democratic Party (HDP) and adopted the slogan 'Everything will be just fine.' Just whether that turns out to be true remains to be seen. The result will boost the confidence of those campaigning for a democratic society and against Erdoğan's autocratic rule, but as a friend from Ankara observed shortly after the result was declared: 'This is the first major defeat for the dictator, and a success for the big coalition of Turkish-Kurdish people and all democratic forces. Restoring democracy will take longer and will need patience.'

## 36 After Istanbul will it be business as usual?

*17 July 2019*

**Not according to a recent briefing by CEFTUS, the UK based Centre for Turkey Studies.**

CEFTUS reported on 11 July that dissidents within the ruling Justice and Development Party (AKP) are on the brink of forming an alternative party, which could deprive the government of its majority in Parliament.

It also reported that a founding member of the AKP has resigned, setting in motion the setting up of a new party. As former Deputy Prime Minister of Turkey responsible for the Economy, Ali Babacan built a reputation as a competent figure trusted by the country's European allies and the markets. He is now understood to be in discussions with other 'moderate' AKP figures, including former Prime Minister Ahmet Davutoğlu and former President Abdullah Gül.

Rumours of a split from within the AKP have intensified since the AKP's defeat in Istanbul last month, which sent shock waves through the ruling party, showing that President Recep Tayyip Erdoğan was no longer a winner. This, plus tensions within the party over Erdoğan's centralisation of power and the failing economy, could represent a serious challenge to his authority.

That's not to say that it's been all change overnight. Journalists and others are still be dragged before the courts. But today there was some good news, when the 13th High Criminal Court in Istanbul acquitted two journalists and a human rights activist of terrorism charges.

Erol Önderoğlu, the Turkey representative for press freedom watchdog Reporters Without Borders (RSF), journalist Ahmet Nesin, and Sebnem Korur Fincanci, chairwoman of Turkey's Human Rights Foundation, had been arrested in June 2016, accused of spreading terrorist propaganda for their work with a Kurdish newspaper, which has since been closed down. But the three maintained they were defending free speech amid a clampdown by President Erdoğan.

Applause erupted in the courtroom as the verdict was read out and the decision was welcomed by the IFJ/EFJ and many other press freedom organisations.

Earlier, the European and International Federations of Journalists (EFJ/IFJ) had called for their acquittal and release. Erol Önderoğlu was facing 14 years and six months in jail over 'terror propaganda'. He was charged because of his participation in 2016 as temporary editor-in-chief to the production of the now-closed Özgür Gündem daily newspaper as part of the Editors in Chief on Watch campaign.

This was a solidarity action organised from May to August 2016 by the now-closed newspaper, a pro-Kurdish rights publication subjected to multiple investigations and lawsuits. Önderoğlu was one of the 56 prominent journalists and activists who acted as 'editor for the day' and published three articles in the daily on 18 May 2016. The campaign was intended to draw attention to the Turkish authorities' attempts to put pressure on the publication and its journalists.

Meanwhile the National Union of Journalists' national executive passed the following motion at its meeting last Friday:

**Journalism in Turkey**
This NEC welcomes the release from prison in Istanbul of Ayşe Düzkan six months into her 18 month sentence for her bogus crimes as a journalist. This NEC notes with regret, however, that she is still being required to undertake unpaid 'community payback' style work.

This NEC notes that by publicising the case of Ayşe Düzkan, and involving branches in the campaign for her release, the NUJ successfully drew attention to the plight of journalists in Turkey. This NEC calls for this work to continue and asks the General Secretary and chair of the Policy Committee to identify another journalist jailed in Turkey that they union can 'adopt'.

This NEC notes that Turkey is still the world's biggest jailer of journalists and that President Erdoğan's assault on Turkey's media continues unabated.

This NEC further notes and condemns the report by the Washington DC-based Foundation for Political Economic and Social Research, or SETA (a think tank with close links to Erdoğan's Justice And Development Party) that has publicly identified reporters working in Turkey for international organisations, and accusing them of bias against the government.

This NEC notes that the journalists named and condemned in the report include reporters from the BBC, Deutsche Welle, Eurovision as well as the Voice of America and others.

This NEC concurs with our sister union the Turkish Union of Journalists, which considers that the report illegally 'recorded personal information' as well as 'inciting people to hatred'.

The NEC calls on the General Secretary to ensure that campaigning to expose the terrible treatment of journalists in Turkey is a prominent feature in our campaigning on international matters.

# Journalism and press freedom

## 37  Moscow revisited
### 24 November 2014

**The annual meeting of the European Federation of Journalists (EFJ) was held last week in Moscow. It was my first visit to Russia since the dramatic and turbulent days of Mikhail Gorbachev in the late 1980s.**

Then, one rouble was worth one pound sterling. Now, £1.40 can buy 100 roubles. That's not all that has changed of course, but that's another story.

We were the guests of the Russian Union of Journalists (RUJ), whose members are facing increasing opposition from the Russian government for their brave stand in defence of ethical, honest and independent journalism. Since 1992, this has cost 58 journalists their lives (see: *https://cpj.org/killed/europe/russia/*), and their pictures hang in the main hall of the union's headquarters in Nikita Boulevard, only a few minutes' drive from the Kremlin and 'Red' (Beautiful) Square, as a grim reminder.

The headquarters (or House of Journalists) is a remarkable building with a wonderful history, which also houses the Moscow Journalists' Club. It was a cultural centre before the 1917 Revolution, and maintains that tradition today, with art exhibitions and book sales as well as being a place for meetings, eating and drinking.

In 1918, the Soviet Union of Journalists was set up here, and Lenin and Trotsky were elected honorary chairs. A bust of Lenin can still be seen at the bottom of the stairs leading to the main hall, where we held our meeting.

During the Stalin era, many writers and journalists became victims of the terror, and the union ceased to function. The Khrushchev 'thaw' led to the union being re-established, but it was totally dominated by the Communist Party and funded by the State.

In the 1980s, a number of independent professional organisations flourished in the USSR, and the independent RUJ was established in 1992.

Three years later, the RUJ joined the International Federation of Journalists (IFJ).

However, the union is under frequent attack by the government and, in August, the then president of the IFJ, Jim Boumelha, wrote to President Putin complaining of the increasing pressure being put on the RUJ, and called for an end to intimidation, which included a threat to evict them from their headquarters. We were told that this threat still hangs over the union.

While we were there, reports came in of yet another attack on independent media in Russia. The country's only 'opposition minded' radio station Ekho Moskvy, a subsidiary of Gazprom, the state controlled gas giant, which holds a controlling stake in the station, was in crisis because of a twitter posting by the station's radio host Alexander Plyushchev in which he commented on the recent death by drowning of the Kremlin chief of staff Sergei Ivanov's 37-year-old son, Alexander Ivanov. Plyushchev wondered whether the 'death of Ivanov's son, who ran over an old lady and sued her son-in-law, is proof of the existence of God/higher justice.' He was referring to an incident in 2005, when a 68-year-old woman was hit by Alexander's car and killed.

Plyushchev was threatened with the sack.

Matters came to a head last Wednesday, but by the evening it was reported on the Moscow Times website that the radio station had 'scored a victory in its struggle to preserve editorial independence' after its state-run corporate owner has revoked an order to fire one of the station's journalists and promised to beef up the chief editor's rights:

*http://www.themoscowtimes.com/news/article/russias-ekho-moskvy-celebrates-victory-as-radio-host-dodges-ax/511510.html*

> 'Editor-in-Chief Alexei Venediktov and head of the state-run Gazprom Media holding Mikhail Lesin reached the agreement during a four-hour meeting on Wednesday,' Venediktov told his radio station later that evening. 'Removing a major bone of contention between the parties, Lesin revoked an earlier order to fire Ekho Moskvy radio host Alexander Plyushchev—a dismissal that critics said contradicted the station's charter, which places the authority to dismiss editorial staff with the editor-in-chief.'

It went on to report that Plyushchev would still face some sanctions over the twitter post at the heart of the dispute.

The post was later deleted and replaced with an apology.

It was later reported that the station has until 25 December to draft amendments to its charter, adding guidelines for using social networks under an agreement with its state-run corporate owner Gazprom.

# 38  After all this time—it's IMPRESS

## 27 October 2016

**The Press Recognition Panel (PRP), established by parliament following the Leveson report published in November 2012, has approved IMPRESS's application for recognition under the Royal Charter.**

At a meeting on Tuesday in a west London hotel (opposite the BBC HQ in Portland Place) the PRP considered, line by line, whether the press regulator met the criteria set out in the charter. After nearly five hours of consideration, witnessed by dozens of members of the public (including me for the morning session) and transmitted live on the Internet, the panel decided that it did.

The decision makes IMPRESS the only press regulator which is Leveson-compliant and one which the public, readers and victims of press abuse can trust to regulate newspapers and safeguard freedom of the press, while offering redress when they get things wrong.

It had been hoped that the decision would be made at the Panel meeting in August, but a letter from the News Media Association (described in the autumn issue 208 of the Campaign for Press and Broadcasting Freedom's magazine as a 'front organisation for the national newspapers') raised further questions on the IMPRESS application.

The same article in Free Press pointed out that: 'The national papers hate IMPRESS (most are quite happy with IPSO, the Independent Press Standards Organisation ...) and seek to derail the process at every stage, which is all too easy.'

IPSO is not Leveson-compliant and has no intention of applying for recognition under the Royal Charter, for the simple reason it would be rejected by the PRP.

So a further round of consultation was undertaken, and the outcome carefully and thoroughly analysed by the panel at its meeting on Tuesday.

The board had every reason to be fastidious. They were obliged to do so under Leveson procedures and the threat of legal action by some national newspaper publishers loomed in the background as a possible challenge to the legality of any decision. That's because the significance of the decision means that newspapers which do not sign up to the regulator could face paying out considerable amounts of money in court cases, by being liable to pay costs for both sides.

As *Private Eye* (28 October—10 November edition) puts it: '... Section 40 of the Crime and Courts Act 2013 will kick in, requiring judges to make news publishers who don't belong to IMPRESS ... pay the costs of people who sue them regardless of whether they win or lose.' However, it's not clear if the government will implement this controversial provision, following heavy lobbying by sections of the industry, so this will be the next campaign target for those supporting the Leveson provisions for an effective, independent press regulator.

Karen Bradley, the Culture Secretary, told a hearing of the Commons select committee the day before IMPRESS was given recognition that the Department for Culture, Media and Sport is still considering the matter. Meanwhile, some newspaper publishers are muttering about a legal challenge to these provisions as being contrary to the European Convention on Human Rights (a piece of legislation they hate and want to see repealed) and want to stick with IPSO.

Quoted in the Mail Online on 25 October, Bob Satchwell, executive director of the Society of Editors, said the decision was 'irrelevant' to the reality of press regulation, adding that the vast majority of the press and significant publishers reject the Royal Charter system under which the PRP was set up.

He added: 'This is an organisation set up by politicians with public funds but it has no real work to do because IMPRESS represents only a very small number of local publishers.'

So, although a significant step has been taken to clean up press regulation in the wake of the phone hacking scandal, and subsequent Leveson report, there are many hurdles ahead. Apart from getting the government to implement section 40, IMPRESS itself needs to sign up more members, a task it can now do with more confidence.

As investigative journalist Nick Davies said in a statement issued by the media reform pressure group Hacked Off:

> No decent journalist wants their work regulated by IPSO—an organisation which is vulnerable to the influence of some very bad people from the worst newspapers in the UK. IMPRESS is a decent alternative, independent of government and of newspapers.
>
> It tells you all you need to know about the continuing scandal of press misbehaviour in the UK that these notorious newspapers will not join a regulator which can be trusted to enforce the code of conduct which they themselves have written and claim to want to honour; and that in spite of overwhelming public and parliamentary support, government is too scared of those newspapers to trigger Section 40, which would put pressure on those newspapers to join such a regulator.

## Update

According to its 2018–19 Annual report, IMPRESS Regulates 142 digital and print publications across the UK reaching more than 10 million readers each month. But the campaign for media reform has suffered some severe setbacks. During this period parliament decided to scrap part two of the Leveson Inquiry, which was to investigate links between the press and the police.

As a result of heavy lobbying by the industry, section 40 of the Crime and Courts Act 2013, was repealed by parliament in May 2019. In response the News Media Association, a trade body which styles itself as 'the voice of national, regional and local news media organisations in the UK', dropped its legal challenge against the Press Recognition Panel over its decision to recognise IMPRESS under the Royal Charter. Small compensation, as it was unlikely that the appeal would have succeeded.

Most of the so-called mainstream media who are members of the News Media Association are 'regulated' by IPSO, described by George Monbiot last December as 'not fit for purpose', and its complaints process which 'seems designed to deter' (Guardian 10 December 2019).

## 39 Election 2017: Tories let press barons off the hook

### 19 May 2017

**This week the two main parties published their election manifestos and their sections on plans for the media make interesting reading.**

Labour is supportive of the BBC and public service broadcasting; of reforming media ownership rules; and continuing the work of the Leveson Inquiry, which has not pleased the media barons.

The Conservatives, by contrast, have thrown the media barons a lifeline by pledging to repeal Section 40 of the Crime and Courts Act 2013, which would give victims of press abuse access to affordable justice. Section 40 provides that in the event a 'relevant publisher' (i.e. a provider of general news in print) is sued, and that publisher has chosen not to register with an 'approved regulator' (i.e. one that is Leveson-compliant), that publisher will be required to pay a claimant's costs even if the publisher wins in court. The provision was recommended by Leveson and supported by parliament in 2013, but would only come into force once an approved regulator was set up (as IMPRESS was in October 2016—see 38: 'After all this time—it's IMPRESS)'. They also pledge to scrap Part 2 of the Leveson Inquiry.

Labour, on the other hand, says:

> The BBC is a national asset which we should all be proud of. Unlike the Conservatives, Labour will always support it and uphold its independence. We will ensure the BBC and public service broadcasting has a healthy future. Labour is committed to keeping Channel 4 in public ownership and will guarantee the future of Welsh-language broadcaster S4C.
>
> Victims of phone hacking have been let down by a Conservative government that promised them justice, but failed to follow through. We will implement the recommendations of Part 1 of the Leveson Inquiry and commence Part 2, which will look into the corporate governance failures that allowed the hacking scandal to occur.
>
> Local newspapers and broadcasting in Britain are an important part of our democracy and culture. We are concerned about closures of local media outlets and the reductions in number of local journalists. Labour will hold a national review (into) local media and into the ownership of national media to ensure plurality.
>
> To protect democracy and media freedom, we will take steps to ensure that Ofcom is better able to safeguard a healthy plurality of media ownership and to put in place clearer rules on who is fit and proper to own or run TV and radio stations.

As mentioned above, Labour pledges to hold Part 2 of the Leveson Inquiry, which has been the source of intensive lobbying against by most of the media owners, who want to shut down any further public debate. And, with the Fox bid for Sky still on the table, any further revelations about the behaviour of News International, on top of the recent reports about the behaviour of top management of Fox in the US, is the last thing Murdoch wants.

It's worth reminding ourselves just what Part 2 is supposed to cover. The terms of reference read:

> To inquire into the extent of unlawful or improper conduct within News International, other newspaper organisations and, as appropriate, other organisations within the media, and by those responsible for holding personal data.
>
> To inquire into the way in which any relevant police force investigated allegations or evidence of unlawful conduct by persons within or connected with News International, the review by the Metropolitan Police of their initial investigation, and the conduct of the prosecuting authorities.

> To inquire into the extent to which the police received corrupt payments or other inducements, or were otherwise complicit in such misconduct or in suppressing its proper investigation, and how this was allowed to happen.
>
> To inquire into the extent of corporate governance and management failures at News International and other newspaper organisations, and the role, if any, of politicians, public servants and others in relation to any failure to investigate wrongdoing at News International.
>
> In the light of these inquiries, to consider the implications for the relationships between newspaper organisations and the police, prosecuting authorities, and relevant regulatory bodies—and to recommend what actions, if any, should be taken.

So, whilst Labour wants to complete Leveson, which should mean that the Fox bid should have to be 'on hold', the Tories have come to their rescue by not only scrapping Leveson Part 2, but by promising to repeal section 40 of the Crimes and Court Act, which is awaiting a decision on implementation following a public consultation held by the Department for Culture, Media and Sport, which closed on 17 January 2017.

Here's what the Conservative Party manifesto says about completing the Leveson Inquiry:

> **A free media**
>
> At a time when the internet is changing the way people obtain their news, we also need to take steps to protect the reliability and objectivity of information that is essential to our democracy and a free and independent press. We will ensure content creators are appropriately rewarded for the content they make available online. We will be consistent in our approach to regulation of online and offline media. Given the comprehensive nature of the first stage of the Leveson Inquiry and given the lengthy investigations by the police and Crown Prosecution Service into alleged wrongdoing, we will not proceed with the second stage of the Leveson Inquiry into the culture, practices and ethics of the press. We will repeal Section 40 of the Crime and Courts Act 2014, which, if enacted, would force media organisations to become members of a flawed regulatory system or risk having to pay the legal costs of both sides in libel and privacy cases, even if they win.

Music to the ears of the media barons!

Brian Cathcart from Hacked Off made a strong point in his article in Inforrm's (The International Forum for Responsible Media) blog of 18 May, when he wrote that a single paragraph on page 80 of the Conservative manifesto promises to 'erase all trace of the Leveson enquiry from public life'. Without Leveson Part 2, he says, it will be 'just as if the world never found out that Rupert Murdoch's company hacked Millie Dowler's phone', leaving us without effective, independent regulation for the press, and ordinary people, unable to afford High Court action, might as well 'whistle for justice' when they are libelled. He sees the policy as 'a carte blanche [to] break the law and behave as unethically as they wish', with only IPSO (a 'feeble sham') to protect them.

The Conservatives, he says, are promising to save the 'Dacres and Murdochs' of this world by waving 'a magic wand' over past criminality, and entering into a pact between newspaper bosses and politicians that exposes thousands of ordinary people to cruelty at the hands of unscrupulous newspapers. 'It is a piece of politics worthy of the very shabbiest banana republic.'

And as for us—now we know what May meant by 'strong and stable government'.

It's keeping on the right side of the press barons.

# 40  It was social media what swung it!

## 15 June 2017

**In a well-argued letter to the Guardian, published on 12 June, Professor James Curran, who writes and lectures on media history and policy, declared that: '... the reign of the tabloids is over.**

'For weeks, the ancient bazookas controlled [by the] press oligarchs were trained on Corbyn and McDonnell, portraying them as patrons of terror and fantasists forever shaking a magic money tree. The campaign failed because the English press is more distrusted than any other in Europe ... and young people ... get their news and political information from the internet ...'

The Tory party campaign was riddled with insults against the Labour leader, too many to mention here, while the press coverage was described by the veteran political journalist Nicholas Jones as the 'vilest general election reporting of my lifetime ...'

Just days before polling, and after the Manchester bombing, with the election slipping away from her, May branded the Labour leader as 'unpatriotic' and 'soft on terror'.

There was even worse in the Sun and Mail, but Corbyn refused to indulge in personal insults. The day before the election, the Mail took up 13 pages denouncing Corbyn, John McDonnell and Diane Abbot as 'apologists for terror'.

So why did the tabloid Tory cheerleaders end up with egg on their faces—and is it really the end of the reign of the tabloids as James Curran suggests?

An answer, as he himself suggested, can be found in two words—social media.

I must confess I am not a follower and had no real idea of its impact until I started talking to some younger people when I was 'knocking up' for John Grogan, the successful Labour in candidate in Keighley, West Yorkshire on election day.

I was also doubtful about the television exit poll on election night, until around 2 a.m. when the real results started to bear it out. It is clear that, although Labour did not win the election, they won the battle for votes via social media.

Young people used YouTube and Facebook to stunning effect and networked with their friends. But we have to remember that it was the party's policies that appealed to younger voters: after all, you need a relevant programme to mobilise them around in the first place. Without it the social media campaigns would have been useless.

While hundreds, if not thousands, turned out to Corbyn's rallies, tens of thousands watched them on YouTube. Labour, on Twitter, with its hashtag *#forthemany* helped deliver the younger vote and increase the party's share of the vote to 40 per cent.

As for the right-wing tabloids (who have now turned on May), they seem down, but by no means out. Rupert Murdoch may have fumed at the result, but May has recalled his boy Gove to the cabinet. And the tabloids still influence the broadcasting and TV news agendas as well as many older voters.

Also, the Tories took votes from Labour in some midland and northern areas that were strong EU leavers.

Then there is the question of Murdoch's bid for the rest of Sky, the futures of Leveson 2 and press regulation.

All this is unfinished business. There's a lot to fight for.

And we can win.

## 41 Journalism under threat but not trusted

### 5 December 2017/May 2018

**'Just when journalists thought legal threats to press freedom in Britain couldn't get any worse, along comes another menacing piece of legislation.'**

So wrote Roy Greenslade, journalist and academic, in the Guardian on 4 December 2017 ('the Data Protection Bill is yet another legal threat to UK press freedom').

He went on to say that, after the 'snooper's charter' (or, as it is officially known, the Investigatory Powers Act) and the proposal by the Law Commission for a new Espionage Act 'that could transform journalism into spying', along comes the Data Protection Bill.

'This bill,' he says, 'now making its way through parliament, has the potential to inhibit investigative journalism. It has alarmed news broadcasters and newspapers alike. Yet thanks to the domination of our media landscape by Brexit, the bill has not received anything like enough attention. That is a grave oversight.'

The bill has been tabled by the Department of Culture and is currently being debated in the House of Lords before it goes to the Commons. According to Greenslade, it would also make life more difficult for whistle-blowers who, like the journalists they contact, risk being criminalised for obtaining and retaining personal data without consent. It would be a further obstacle in getting people to come forward and provide valuable information about corruption and other wrong-doing.

Meanwhile the Press Gazette has recently reported the result of a poll conducted by the Ipsos Mori Veracity Index which found that UK journalists are less trusted than estate agents. Just 27 per cent of those surveyed trust journalists to tell the truth. Only politicians (17 per cent) ranked lower in the annual October survey, which questioned 998 adults. Nurses got the best rating at 94 per cent.

It's an improvement since the survey first began in 1983. Then only 17 per cent of Britons trusted journalists to tell them the truth. In 1993 trust in journalists hit a low point of 12 per cent, but has improved since the hacking scandal of 2011 when the survey found trust has risen to 21 per cent. Television journalists scored better, with a 38 per cent trust rating (more than priests, who came out at 35 per cent).

Earlier research found that UK newspapers were the least trusted in Europe.

A recent report for Reuters' Institute for the Study of Journalism found that the main reasons for distrust were bias, exaggeration, sensationalism and low standards.

Now, six months later, a report published by the US Pew Research Center has found that less than half the adults in the UK say that the news media is doing a good job at getting the facts right: the worst trustworthiness rate in Western Europe.

The report was published at the same time that the House of Commons rejected the call to hold Part 2 of the Leveson Inquiry into the conduct of the media. This was to include a number of new provisions among which was an investigation into the dissemination of information and news, including false news stories.

The Research Center asked a total of 16,000 people across the UK, Denmark, France, Germany, Italy, Netherlands, Spain and Sweden about their views on the media, and their use of social media to get news. Each country had roughly 2,000 respondents, who were surveyed between last October and December (2017).

The UK was rated joint second worst for investigating the actions of its government, tying with France on 51 per cent. Italy rated worse on 42 per cent who thought they were doing a good job.

The UK was also second worst for being politically neutral in its news coverage, with only 37 per cent believing that their press was doing a good job. This is hardly surprising, as newspapers (unlike broadcasters) have no obligation to present balanced coverage. Only 48 per cent thought the UK media were doing a good job at 'getting the facts right'. This was the lowest figure, with Italy and Spain closest, at 55 per cent. Although better trusted for covering the economy (65 per cent) and crime (70 per cent), it was the least trusted on its coverage of immigration (44 per cent).

The report also covered the use of social media as a news source, finding that the majority of people get their news from social media 'at least sometimes', with 38 per cent doing so daily.

*See: http://pressgazette.co.uk/uk-news-media-least-trusted-among-eight-european-nations-to-get-the-facts-right-and-cover-important-stories-of-the-day-report-shows/*
*Sources: Pew Research Center and Charlotte Tobitt Press Gazette 15 May 2018*

## 42 Press freedom plunges world-wide
### 7 December 2017

**Global media freedom is at its lowest level for ten years according to a study by a freedom of expression organisation ARTICLE 19.**

The study was undertaken with the social science database V-Dem to launch a unique, authoritative assessment of freedom of expression and information worldwide. It examined the state of freedom of expression in 172 countries.

Its report points out that: 'The United Kingdom has passed one of the most draconian surveillance legislation of any democracy, offering a template for authoritarian regimes and seriously undermining the rights of its citizens to privacy and freedom of expression.'

In Turkey, 'the data indicate that transparency peaked in 2003, the year that the law on the right to information was adopted, and has declined significantly ever since, now down to almost the level following the 1980 coup.'

According to the IFJ/EFJ, more than 120 journalists are in jail or on trial in Turkey, over 200 media outlets have been closed down and nearly 3,000 employees in the media sector have been left without jobs. Withdrawal of press cards, cancellation of passports and seizure of assets have become almost daily routine.

The report's key findings are that:

• Global media freedom is at its lowest level for ten years. In 2016 alone, 259 journalists were imprisoned worldwide, and 79 were killed.

• Internet censorship has become more pervasive since 2006 (the year that Twitter was launched, and Facebook and YouTube were still in their infancy). Algorithms are increasingly used to remove legal and illegal content with little transparency over the process or consideration of human rights.

• Much of the world's online content is now regulated by the community standards of a handful of internet companies, whose processes lack transparency and are not subject to the checks and balances of traditional governance. Private communications are being subject to surveillance as never before, as states, including the UK, pass legislation to enable extensive digital surveillance.

• Governments are using unprecedented legal and other measures to silence dissenting voices and protest by individuals and civil society organisations. These tactics include labelling NGOs as 'foreign agents' and the illegal surveillance of NGOs and journalists.

The call for greater transparency is one of the most significant positive shifts over the past decades, with right to information laws now in 119 countries.

ARTICLE 19's Executive Director Thomas Hughes commented:

> For the first time, we have a comprehensive and holistic overview of the state of free of expression and information around the world. Unfortunately, our findings show that freedom of expression is under attack in democracies as well as authoritarian regimes ... (a) shift in advertising revenues towards the internet has radically altered traditional media companies. Redundancies, cutbacks and the decline in salaried journalists are contributing to concerns about the future of accurate and reliable journalism in the 21st century. The control of information is increasingly in the hands of a few companies with search engines and algorithms now responsible for delivering news and information to digital audiences, and especially those using social media platforms.

### *Update*

*ARTICLE 19's 2018/19 Global Expression Report (https://www.article19.org/xpa-2019/) found matters even worse reporting that freedom of expression had reached a ten-year low around the world.*

*Increases in threats made towards journalists and in 'digital authoritarianism', government increases in online surveillance and clampdown on content, had all contributed to the downward trend.*

*Sixty-six countries, with a combined population of more than 5.5 bn people, saw their freedom of expression reduce in the past decade. There is less media freedom and digital freedom of expression now than a decade ago in every region of the world except the Middle East and North Africa, it added.*

## 43 Will the NUJ be the first union to recruit robots?

*15 December 2017/Spring 2020*

**Newspapers have started publishing articles jointly written by robots and humans according to a report written by Tom Horton (not a robot) in the Financial Times ('Rise of the machines extends to news reports', 13 December 2017).**

Funded by Google's Digital News Initiative, the Reporters and Data Robots (Radar) with the Press Association and Urbs Media have created software 'which inserts localised statistics into stories written by human reporters.'

Articles of this kind are being offered in a pilot scheme to editors of 35 regional newspapers and, so far, they have appeared in 20 publications. Radar has a future target of 30,000 monthly stories.

The development has been described as a potential 'game-changer' by Toby Granville, editorial development director at Newsquest, the nationwide newspaper group which has been quick to publish part automated stories.

Newsquest has form when it comes to cutting jobs and titles while boardroom remuneration runs to millions.

In a statement on 1 December 2017 ('Newsquest Christmas cuts and redundancy as boss pockets £1m-plus') the NUJ said:

> Newsquest's chief executive Henry Faure Walker's pay and perks have passed the one million pound mark, but scores of journalists face being made redundant just in time for Christmas. Others have been told their meagre overtime and anti-social hours payments will be pared down.
>
> Newspapers throughout the group have been told jobs will go and payments for working bank holidays and weekends and mileage rates will be cut. This follows a year of job losses, title closures and cuts, which have all taken their toll on staff, as a group-wide stress survey has shown. [NUJ] reps said the latest round was potentially hazardous to health—both physically and mentally.

None of this seems to bother Newsquest, which refuses to consult the union on a national level, despite it being obvious that all its newspapers are controlled centrally by the group.

The Financial Times reports NUJ General Secretary Michelle Stanistreet as describing the 'robot' software 'as a useful tool' adding that: 'Ultimately it is the journalist who must check the context and analysis … I cannot see how it could be used to replace journalists.

Humans are still required to make ethical decisions on what is published.'

Quite so, but as with the introduction of 'new technology' in the 1970s, the questions are: who benefits and how is change managed—and in whose interests?

Today technology advances are rapid, and newspapers owners are only too willing to get rid of journalists to cut costs and improve profit margins. Whilst there are no plans for the NUJ to recruit robots, their introduction could pose a further serious threat to jobs and standards in an industry where both have been under attack for many years.

The Newsquest November cull has become such a regular feature that it has been given its own festive hashtag of #Scroogequest

Union reps met on Monday 27 November to discuss the situation. One rep called the latest round of cuts 'insane', since it will be impossible for the remaining staff to take on the extra work.

## *Update*

*In the spring of 2020 it was reported that Microsoft had sacked dozens of journalists after the company had decided to replace them with artificial intelligence software.*

*Staff who maintained the news homepages on Microsoft's MSN website and its Edge browser, used by millions every day, were told that they were no longer required because robots can do their jobs.*

*Some 27 staff employed by PA Media (formerly the Press Association) were subsequently sacked after Microsoft decided to stop employing people to select, edit and curate news articles on its homepages.*

## 44  21st Century Fox proposed Sky takeover—don't let Murdoch snatch victory from the jaws of defeat

*8 February 2018/October 2018*

**Last month the Competition and Markets Authority (CMA) provisionally rejected Rupert Murdoch's £11.7 billion takeover bid for Sky on the grounds that it would give him too much control over the UK media scene and was not in the public interest.**

They did not, however, go for an outright rejection, and any final decision will be taken by the new Culture Secretary, Matt Hancock, in May.

What's more, they did not accept concerns expressed that the new Murdoch-controlled company would not be committed to broadcasting standards. This was despite the phone-hacking scandal at the then Murdoch-owned News of the World, or those about allegations of sexual harassment at Fox News in the US, which is controlled by the Murdoch family trust.

However they threw him a lifeline by offering suggestions as to how Fox (i.e. Murdoch) could address its concerns about media plurality which are now the subject of public consultation.

These are essentially 'behavioural' changes aimed at protecting Sky News from the direct influence of the Murdoch family trust, which included selling or spinning off Sky News altogether.

The news was music to ears of the shareholders. Graham Ruddick, at the Observer (Business) reported on 28 January that on the day of the CMA's announcement shares rose 'as investors and traders betted that the watchdog's deal was more likely to go through …' Ruddick went on to explain that 'This is because it is easier to allay concerns about media plurality—such as by selling off Sky News—than any concerns about broadcasting standards due to the phone hacking scandal at the News of the World, or sexual harassment allegations at Fox News.'

Along with other campaigners, the Campaign for Broadcasting Freedom (CPBF) welcomed the CMA's provisional rejection of Murdoch's bid, but we should never underestimate his ability to turn such a situation to his advantage. Aided by the competition authority's lifeline, his people are working around the clock to convince the CMA to wave through the takeover. We need to continue to mobilise public and political opposition to Murdoch to ensure that the Culture Secretary Matt Hancock blocks the deal.

**Update: Murdoch fails**
*In September, Murdoch failed to gain full control of Sky after Comcast, the largest cable operator in the US, beat Fox with a £30bn bid. The US telecommunications giant won out in a day-long auction overseen by the Takeover Panel.*

*Comcast offered £17.28 per share compared to 21st Century Fox's £15.67 per share for the 61 per cent of the company it does not already own. This failure is a great setback for Murdoch.*

*The following month, NUJ General Secretary, Michelle Stanistreet, reported that she and other trade union leaders were to meet Comcast management and the priority will be gaining access to the 18,000 people working there, and ending the decades-long culture of union hostility.*

*The NUJ would be stepping up the recruitment work that has been taking place throughout the summer.*

# 45 Tory MP climbs down over the spy who never was

## 24 February 2018

**Ben Bradley MP, a Tory party vice-chair who made the claim in a Twitter message to his 4,000 plus followers, which he subsequently deleted, that Jeremy Corbyn sold British secrets to 'communist spies' has made an apology and a donation to charity.**

This should comes as no surprise, as the claim had no substance. The apology was welcomed by Labour, who said the donation would be split between a homeless centre and a food bank in Bradley's constituency of Mansfield.

According to a report on today's Guardian website, Labour said Bradley will tweet an apology that will say: 'On 19 February 2018 I made a seriously defamatory statement on my Twitter account, "Ben Bradley MP (bbradleymp)", about Jeremy Corbyn, alleging he sold British secrets to communist spies. I have since deleted the defamatory tweet. I have agreed to pay an undisclosed substantial sum of money to a charity of his choice, and I will also pay his legal costs.

'I fully accept that my statement was wholly untrue and false. I accept that I caused distress and upset to Jeremy Corbyn by my untrue and false allegations, suggesting he had betrayed his country by collaborating with foreign spies.

'I am very sorry for publishing this untrue and false statement and I have no hesitation in offering my unreserved and unconditional apology to Jeremy Corbyn for the distress I have caused him.'

The tweet was so outrageous that earlier this week Andrew Neil slammed the claims of Conservative MPs that Jeremy Corbyn 'sold British secrets' and 'betrayed his country' on the BBC's Daily Politics television programme.

The smearing of Labour leaders in this way is, of course, nothing new and goes back all the way to 1924 with the Daily Mail's 'Zinoviev letter', a forgery which portrayed Labour as secret agents of the Russian Bolsheviks.

In his response to the current attempted smear, Jeremy Corbyn was spot on when he said that much of our press was not very free at all, being controlled by billionaire tax exiles, and that: 'We've got news for them. Change is coming.'

This latest attempt to discredit a leader of the Labour Party reminds me of a similar smear made in 1995 by the Murdoch press against Michael Foot (leader between 1980 and 83) which ended up in the High Court and the payment of substantial damages. In July of that year, the Sunday Times was forced into a humiliating climb-down over its allegations that Michael Foot was considered an 'agent of influence' by the KGB. The story alleged that Foot had operated under the code name 'Boot' and that the Soviet intelligence service made cash payments to the left-wing journal Tribune while he was editor.

Under a settlement, the paper offered Foot 'substantial' damages—which, with legal costs, were believed to run to at least £100,000—and an assurance that it had never intended to suggest that Foot had been a spy. Earlier the News of the World who also printed the story settled out of court. The sum was reported to be £35,000.

Some of the damages went to Tribune, and he and his legal team celebrated their victory at the Gay Hussar, the Soho restaurant in which alleged 'Agent Boot' met his KGB contacts.

Foot said that: 'If he [Mr Murdoch] owns newspapers which can make accusations of this nature, he should appear in court when they are raised.'

So if Jeremy Corbyn does decide to follow the example of his predecessor, can we expect an appearance by Rupert Murdoch in the courtroom, along with some of the other media mogul tax exiles who are voices of the reactionary right-wing press?

Meanwhile it will be interesting to read how the right-wing press including The Sun and the Mail who did so much to promote the smear, report Bradley's apology. Or will we see them in court?

# 46  The Cairncross Review—can it reverse the decline of local and regional press?

*8 July 2018*

**In March the government commissioned the Cairncross Review to look into the sustainability of high-quality journalism, and threats to journalism, brought about by technological change and consumer behaviour.**

The Review headed by its chair, Frances Cairncross, stated: 'This … is not about preserving the status quo. We need to explore ways in which we can ensure that consumers in 10 years time have access to high-quality journalism which meets their needs, is delivered in the way they want, and supports democratic engagement.'

To do this she recruited an 11-strong advisory panel, which was sharply criticised by the NUJ General Secretary Michelle Stanistreet who pointed out that. 'None of those named represent journalists on the ground who can explain exactly the effect of the present troubles in the industry are having on their ability to produce quality journalism and connect with their communities. We hope Matt Hancock can ensure that the journalist's voice is heard during the process.'

Roy Greenslade also pointed out in the Guardian on 1 July ('Last chance to fill in the blanks on funding journalism future') that 'the panel includes publishers who have been responsible for journalism's deterioration, and who have a vested interested in making profits rather than aiding democracy.'

The Review and its terms of reference were also attacked by Brian Cathcart writing in the Inforrm Blog on 31 March as; '… little more than a device to help him (the Culture Secretary) justify giving fresh public subsidies to his friends and supporters in the corporate press.' He insisted that any money raised as tax was public money and that the idea that this might find its way into the pockets of Rupert Murdoch, Lord Rothermere, the Barclay brothers or the people who run the Mirror and Express was unacceptable.'

See: https://inforrm.org/2018/03/31/the-cairncross-review-its-about-subsidising-the-press-brian-cathcart/#more-39637

Some three months later, the Culture Department published the results of its 90-page investigation (the Mediatique report) as background material for the Review, which found that (surprise, surprise): 'The number of frontline print journalists has dropped by more than a quarter—from 23,000 in 2007 to 17,000 in 2017—and circulation and print advertising revenues have dropped by more than half over the same period.'

And again Culture Secretary Matt Hancock said he was particularly troubled by the movement of local and classified advertising to online, which has contributed to the closure of more than 300 local and regional titles since 2007—raising the prospect (already a reality for many) of communities being left without local news provision. Circulation of regional and local newspapers was also down in the same period by 51 per cent from 63.4 million to 31.4 million.

The NUJ and many other media commentators have been banging on about this for years.

We all know the problems, including the increasing concentration of press ownership locally and regionally, but what about possible solutions? Many press publishers see Cairncross as a way of taxing the highly profitable internet companies such as Facebook and Google and shoving the money their way. But would this ensure that the public gets access to high-quality journalism, which, in Cairncross's words, 'meets their needs, is delivered in the way they want, and supports democratic engagement'?

In addition to the question of increasing ownership concentration, there is also the serious of question of the public's trust in journalism, which needs to be addressed.

A report published by the US Pew Research Center in May found that fewer than half the adults in the UK say that the news media is doing a good job at getting the facts right.

One recent attempt to improve local news-gathering was the decision of government to force the BBC via the licence fee, to fund 150 'local democracy reporters'. This form of subsidy goes to the very media owners who in the past failed to invest in the future of local news, putting profits before good quality journalism, and shareholders' interests before the public interest. They are only too happy to take advantage of the scheme and are even thought to be lobbying for more (while BBC budgets are cut back).

However, it is unlikely that this will lead to any increase in advertising revenue for the press, which has fallen by half over the past decade. Although often protesting in the past that public subsidy was a threat to press freedom, media owners themselves threaten that very freedom by putting profits first.

If one accepts that public subsidy is necessary to save local news from further decline, questions about just what sort of models we should look to for guidance, who should get such support and under what terms, are ones that Cairncross should examine, as are the points made by Brian Cathcart and Roy Greenslade quoted earlier.

In the past, the NUJ has called for an economic stimulus plan for journalism with action aimed at encouraging a variety of voices across all platforms, a greater plurality, maximised through a combination of different models—commercial, public, mutual, employee, co-operative, for profit and not for profit. New media could be stimulated through public support in the form of start-up grants, subsidised technology or training grants, solutions driven by journalists and communities themselves—online radio, broadband, TV, print and online. This would be supported by tax breaks for local media which meet clearly defined public purposes (journalism as a service to the public) and tax credits for individuals subscribing to publications that meet such public purposes. Clear and enforceable conditions need to be applied that safeguard the production of original content in the public interest. There are already a number of local innovatory initiatives like Bureau Local, a collaborative, investigative journalism network producing local, data-driven, public-interest journalism to support, reinvigorate and innovate accountability reporting across the UK (see Gareth Davies, 'The story is in the numbers'—British Journalism Review June 2018). These ideas need to be seriously examined by Cairncross.

But in the end it all comes down to having the political will to make the changes that are necessary to recreate journalism as a public service and bring about a better media not based on failed market models, but one which holds power to account and empowers citizens to participate more fully in society.

## 47 Academic report critical of media coverage of Labour's anti-semitism debate

### 22 October 2018/May 2020

**It's been a hot summer, especially for the Labour leader Jeremy Corbyn, over his handling of alleged anti-semitism in the party and its adoption of the International Holocaust Remembrance Alliance's (IHRA) definition of anti-semitism—together with examples.**

At its height, the dispute dominated the media and it is the way the media covered this controversy that has been the subject of an in-depth, academic-level research by the London-based Media Reform Coalition (MRC). The report can be read at: http://www.mediareform.org.uk/wp-content/uploads/2018/09/Labour-antisemitism-and-the-news-FINAL-PROOFED.pdf.

Although published last month, the report has received little coverage in the mainstream media, but it has been given prominence in the daily socialist newspaper, the Morning Star.

Perhaps this 'blackout' is not surprising when you read the report's main findings which: 'identified myriad inaccuracies and distortions in online and television news, including marked skews in sourcing, omission of essential context or right of reply, misquotation, and false assertions made either by journalists themselves or sources whose contentious claims were neither challenged nor countered.'

Ever since his surprise election as Labour leader in 2015, (and re-election a year later) Jeremy Corbyn has been given a rough ride by the media. In the spring 2018 edition 214 of the Campaign for Press and Broadcasting Freedom's journal Free Press, editor Tim Gopsill tracked the right-wing press attempts to destroy the Labour Party's revival (https://www.cpbf.org.uk/wp-content/uploads/2018/03/FP214.pdf), with headlines such as 'Jezza's Jihadi Comrades' (the Sun) and the Daily Mail attacks on his supposed support for terrorism. The Sun even ran a story 'Corbyn and the Commie Spy', which Gopsill described as 'the fantasies of a minor Czech intelligence functionary of the 1980s, as if they had unearthed a top-secret plot'. This nonsense was trumped by what appeared in The Times on 15 September 2018, which dug up the old discredited story, that another Labour leader, the late Michael Foot, was a paid Soviet informer; discredited because Foot in July 1993 had successfully sued The Sunday Times over a story that the KGB believed him (MF) to have been 'an agent of influence'.

But back to media's coverage of the row about anti-semitism in the Labour Party.

The Media Reform Coalition's report concludes about sourcing of stories that 'both quantitative and qualitative analysis of sourcing revealed marked skews which effectively gave those attacking Labour's revised (anti-semitism) code and championing the IHRA definition a virtually exclusive and unchallenged platform to air their views ... By comparison, their detractors—including a number of Jewish organisations and representatives of other affected minorities—were systematically marginalised from the coverage.'

It is worth noting that lawyer Stephen Sedley, visiting professor at the University of Oxford and a former judge of the court of appeal of England and Wales, pointed out that the UK government, which had adopted the IHRA 'working definition' and the examples, had been warned by the Commons Home Affairs Select Committee in October 2016 that, in the interests of free speech, it ought to adopt an explicit rider that, without additional evidence to suggest anti-semitic intent, it is not anti-semitic to criticise the government of Israel, or to hold the Israeli government to the same standards as other liberal democracies.

'This was ignored,' he wrote in a Guardian panel discussion on 'How should anti-semitism be defined?' https://www.theguardian.com/commentisfree/2018/jul/27/antisemitism-ihra-definition-jewish-writers.

The issues of free speech and freedom of expression are central to this question, but this aspect was not recognised by much of the media.

These arguments may seem to be settled for the time being, (although there are many individual disciplinary cases of alleged anti-semitism by members still to be processed by the party) but the right wing media's hostility to the Labour Party, its policies and leadership have been with us for decades and will always be so.

Hostility to Labour dates back to the leaking of the 'Zinoviev letter' by the security services to the Daily Mail four days before the 1924 general election, when the newspaper splashed headlines across its front page claiming: 'Civil War Plot by Socialists' Masters: Moscow Orders To Our Reds; Great Plot Disclosed.'

Labour lost by a landslide.

The need for accurate and fair reporting highlighted by the MRC report are critical in the interest of democracy and informed public debate. Sections of the media, especially the partisan press, will never accurately report the Labour Party, which is why we need to monitor and challenge their distortions and look to build an independent media more reflective of our society and its diversity.

**Update**
Since this article was written, the Glasgow Media Group has published Bad News For Labour: Antisemitism, the Party and Public Belief *(Pluto Press, October 2019).*

The authors draw on carefully compiled research to reveal interesting findings in this guide to what really lies behind the headlines.

Ken Loach describes it as: 'A book that rigorously examines the facts.'

Also, see 'Labour, Antisemitism and the Media' in: It's the Media, Stupid: The Media, the 2019 Election and the Aftermath, edited by Granville Williams, May 2020, CPBF/North.

# 48 Murdered with impunity
## 14 November 2018/October 2020

**It's some six weeks since the brutal murder in the Saudi consulate in Istanbul of Jamal Khashoggi, the Washington Post columnist, in what, on the basis of the evidence so far, was a state-sponsored killing.**

To date, the Saudi ruling elite, in the person of Crown Prince Mohammed bin Salman, claim to know nothing of the atrocity, but they have arrested 18 people who are alleged to have been involved in the operation.

A veteran journalist, Jamal had worked for various Saudi news organisations, covering major stories, including the Soviet invasion of Afghanistan and the rise of Osama Bin Laden. He was close to the Saudi royal family for decades and had been editor-in-chief of the Saudi newspaper Al Watan and a media adviser to Prince Turki al-Faisal, Saudi Arabia's ambassador to Britain.

But he fell out of favour and went into self-imposed exile in the United States in September 2017. From there he wrote a monthly column in the Washington Post, in which he criticised the policies of Crown Prince Mohammed bin Salman (MBS), especially following the actions of the Saudi security services who arrested scores of prominent businessmen and imprisoned them inside the Ritz-Carlton under the cover of an 'anti-corruption' crackdown. In reality it was an operation to frighten off potential rivals. According to Gabriel Sherman writing in Vanity Fair on 16 October 2018 (*https://www.vanityfair.com/news/2018/10/how-jamal-khashoggi-fell-out-with-bin-salman*), Khashoggi soon began hearing from friends in Saudi Arabia that prisoners were coerced, in some cases by torture, into turning over billions of dollars to the government.

'It was tough. Some were insulted. Some were hit. Some claim they were electrocuted,' he said.

The purge, which also included intellectuals, media personalities, and moderate clerics, convinced Khashoggi that MBS had sold himself as a reformer when in fact he was a brutal authoritarian.

'When the arrests started happening, I flipped. I decided it was time to speak,' he told Sherman.

Shortly after his death, a whispering campaign started against him inside Saudi Arabia that Khashoggi was a Muslim Brotherhood supporter, a point also laboured in articles by Saudi sympathisers. In 2014 the Brotherhood was banned in the Saudi kingdom, where it is regarded as a terrorist organisation. There does not appear to be any doubt that he joined the Brotherhood early in his career and that his attraction to political Islam later helped him forge a personal bond with President Recep Tayyip Erdoğan, himself no friend of critical journalism in Turkey where some 90 journalists are in jail.

But, in the end, we are defending freedom of expression even if we have political differences.

It was against this background that the International Federation of Journalists (IFJ) recently launched its campaign against impunity (#endimpunity campaign 2018). The Federation points out that impunity occurs when threats, attacks and crimes against journalists go unpunished. It results in a high level of fear, intimidation, censorship and self-censorship that undermines press freedom, the public right to know and leaves victims and their relatives powerless.

According to IFJ statistics, since the beginning of 2018, at least 75 journalists have lost their lives while carrying out their duties. To date only one out of 10 killings of journalists is resolved. The situation for non-fatal attacks on journalists is even worse.

Governments fail in their duty to hunt down the harassers, the attackers, the killers of media workers. Impunity not only endangers journalists, it imperils democracy and compromises hopes for peace and development. Legal guarantees exist for the protection of journalists as civilians which states are duty bound to enforce under domestic and international law.

The campaign: (*https://www.ifj.org/actions/ifj-campaigns/campaign-against-impunity-2018.html*) aims to hold governments and de facto governments accountable for their impunity records and to denounce crimes targeting journalists that remain unpunished.

Murder is the worst form of these crimes but all attacks targeting journalists that remain unpunished must be exposed and acted upon. According to the IFJ, in the past six years, more than 600 journalists have been killed—and 75 so far in 2018.

One month after the murder of Jamal Khashoggi, 2 November, marked the 'International Day to End Impunity for Crimes against Journalists'. The Safety of Journalists Platform launched a special page, presenting 16 cases of unsolved murders of journalists in the Council of Europe member states. These were submitted by the partner organisations, including the European Federation of Journalists (EFJ) and the IFJ. These cases are listed on the platform as impunity for murders, highlighting deficiencies in investigations and failure to bring to justice all the perpetrators, the organisers or the masterminds of these crimes. See: (*https://www.coe.int/en/web/media-freedom/home*).

In recent years, journalists have been murdered in Malta, Turkey, Ukraine, Serbia and Russia, while many face repressive laws, death threats, physical attacks, arrests and other forms of harassment. Journalists are increasingly being targeted by those who want to silence the messenger and crush debate and the public right to know.

It's time to step up our efforts to campaign for greater media freedom and the right to report. Failure is not an option, there is too much at stake.

## Update

*On Friday 2 October 2020, the National Press Club in Washington held a moment of silence in observance of the second anniversary of the murder of Saudi journalist and Washington Post Global Opinions contributing columnist Jamal Khashoggi.*

*A month earlier it was reported that a Saudi court had overturned five death sentences over his murder, in a final ruling that jailed eight defendants for between seven and 20 years, state media reported.*

*'Five of the convicts were given 20 years in prison and another three were jailed for seven to 10 years,' the official Saudi Press Agency said, citing a spokesman for the public prosecutor.*

*None of the defendants was named.*

Meanwhile, just days before the second anniversary, Turkish prosecutors indicted six new Saudis suspected of involvement in the 2018 murder of Jamal Khashoggi. Istanbul prosecutors are seeking life imprisonment for two of the suspects and up to five years in jail for the remaining four, the official Turkish Anadolu news agency reported.

The six suspects are not in Turkey and are likely to be tried 'in absentia'.

# 49 No happy new year for them!

## 7 January 2019

**The change of year has not meant a change of circumstances for the 177 journalists who, according to the European Federation of Journalists (EFJ), spent New Year's Eve in prison.**

Following reports from the EFJ national affiliates, 177 journalists in Europe spent New Year's Eve in prison: 159 in Turkey; 11 in Azerbaijan; five in Russia; two in Ukraine.

In Turkey, a significant number of journalists continue to be detained on charges related to alleged terrorism, while others convicted in 2018 received heavy prison sentences, including life. According to the EFJ, no progress has been recorded about journalists currently serving life imprisonment or very long sentences, and they have issued a strong call for release of all imprisoned journalists in Europe.

The Federation also identified different forms of judicial harassment aimed at journalists, preventing them from playing their role as public watch-dogs. These included arrests and short-term detentions during protests and demonstrations, or while covering public events or investigating police links to illegal traffickers.

The EFJ reported such cases in Greece, Belgium, Germany, and Italy while criminal charges against journalists for alleged misuse of personal information were reported in Hungary. In Russia and Azerbaijan, complaints were lodged before the domestic courts by the authorities seeking jail sentences for journalists on apparently trumped-up charges, such as extortion or theft. Charges against journalists for disclosure of confidential information were reported in Spain and the United Kingdom.

Meanwhile, at the end of 2018 the International Federation of

Journalists (IFJ) published a list of 94 journalists and media staff killed in work-related incidents during the year. The death-toll marks a slight increase from the 82 killings recorded in 2017 and represents a reversal of the downward trend from the previous three years.

In Europe, four journalists were killed in 2018: Jan Kuciak (Slovakia), Jamal Kashoggi (Turkey) (see 48 'Murdered with Impunity'), Victoria Marinova (Bulgaria), and Antonio Megalizzi (France). The list does not include the Russian journalist Maksim Borodin who died in suspicious circumstances in Ekaterinburg (Russia).

The IFJ says that last year's roll-call of lives lost worldwide by violence, includes 84 journalists, camera operatives, fixers and technicians who died in targeted killings, bomb attacks and cross-fire incidents. Ten other media staff members who worked as drivers, protection officers and a sales assistant also lost their lives. There were six women among the 94 victims. There were also three other work-related deaths.

According to IFJ's 2018 records, the Asia-Pacific region had the highest death tally with 32, followed by the Americas with 27 killings, the Middle East and the Arab World recording 20. Africa came fourth with eleven killings, with Europe with four.

*Source, EFJ website at:*
*https://europeanjournalists.org/*

## 50  Public money needed to save local journalism says Cairncross

### *20 February 2019/January 2020*

**Almost a year ago, the government announced the setting up of a commission chaired by Dame Frances Cairncross to examine the future of local journalism.**

The commission reported earlier this month. Its purpose was to look into the sustainability of high-quality journalism, and threats to journalism brought about by technological change and consumer behaviour. (See 46 'The Cairncross Review—can it reverse the decline of local and regional press?')

After the commission was set up and the panel of advisers selected, Cairncross was allowed just ten weeks (which included the August holiday period) for public consultation. Despite this short time, the commission received 757 responses. Among those media-related organisations giving evidence were the Campaign for Press and Broadcasting Freedom (now closed down), the Ethical Journalists' Network, Hacked Off, the press regulator IMPRESS, the Media Reform Coalition (MRC), the MediaWise Trust and the National Union of Journalists (NUJ).

Evidence was also received from publishers, advertising organisations, platforms/tech companies, journalists (12), academics (24), non-media bodies/charities, public service broadcasters and two 'others'. The panel also met with organisations and individuals.

The report, published on 12 February, echoed many concerns already raised by interested parties about the future of the newspaper industry. It did so repeating the belief that the closure of local newspapers threatened democracy and noted that many local newspapers were owned by debt-ridden publishers who had cut investment and sacked hundreds of journalists in order to maintain profits. This had brought about a crisis in the coverage of local democracy.

The report continued, 'The cost of investigative journalism is great and rarely seems to pay for itself ... given the evidence of market failure in the supply of public-interest news, public intervention may be the only remedy.'

An important contributory factor to the broken economic model was the shift of classified advertising revenue away from local publications to on-line advertising. The report noted that advertising revenue placed by small businesses with the three largest regional publishing companies fell from £2.8bn to £832m in the decade to 2016.

## *Recommendations*

Dame Frances's report made nine recommendations which included:

• Direct funding for public-interest news outlets, with public funds used to support reporting of local democracy through a new institute of public interest news

• An investigation by the competition regulator into the online advertising marketplace, which would consider whether Google's and Facebook's position is too dominant.

• A new code of conduct between publishers and large technology companies, overseen by a regulator which would ensure tech firms treat news publishers fairly.

• Tax relief for publishers which invest in public interest journalism, potentially by giving charitable status to some publishers.

- Removing the 20 per cent VAT tax on digital news subscriptions, bringing online paywalls in line with printed newspapers.

Other recommendations included an Ofcom review of the BBC's market impact and a call for the government to develop a media literacy strategy.

### *Reactions*

Reactions to the report from media reformers were generally supportive, but critical of some recommendations. Writing in the Inforrm Blog, Professor of Communications at Westminster University, Steven Barnett, said that the report '... has produced some innovative and potentially exciting ideas which—if properly and independently implemented—could genuinely deliver more diverse, high-quality public interest journalism, particularly at the local level, where it is desperately needed. But it will require political will to resist a powerful print lobby motivated by corporate self interest ...'

Natham Sparks, Policy Director of Hacked Off, said: 'Cairncross has made some welcome and positive proposals, but she has ducked the two greatest threats to the future of the press in the UK: collapse in public trust, and the power of the publishers. Without addressing these two existential threats to the UK press industry, the recommendations published today will have little effect.'

Professor of Journalism at Kingston University, Surrey, Brian Cathcart, said: 'It makes decent proposals for helping public service journalism but they are worryingly vulnerable to manipulation by corporate press bosses and their ministerial friends ...'

The Media Reform Coalition's (MRC) Angela Phillips welcomed the report's conclusion that support for public-interest news providers was particularly urgent and justified and that government should look to plug the local gap to ensure the continued supply of local democracy reporting and: 'Given the evidence of a market failure in the supply of public-interest news, public intervention may be the only remedy.'

NUJ General Secretary Michelle Stanistreet said: 'Dame Frances Cairncross's report is an important piece of work which charts the demise of local journalism, the cuts to newsrooms and the loss of titles largely because of the move to digital, with people reading their news on the tech giants' platforms, and the draining of advertising revenue to Facebook and Google. The tax concessions and other measures are to be welcomed, but I hope this has not been a missed opportunity.'

Turning to the report's comments on the BBC she said: 'Seeing the BBC served up once again as a bogeyman and convenient cash cow is also an affront to the vital role of public service broadcasting in our democracy and its massive contribution to the broader creative industries. The BBC already funds the local democracy reporter scheme and its technical innovations such as the iPlayer led the way and have been used by other broadcasters. It's a nonsense to suggest that BBC online has destroyed local newspapers—as the report says, the newspaper groups went on costly acquisition sprees before the market collapsed in the late 2000s and then cut investment and sacked hundreds of journalists to maintain profit margins.'

Welcoming the report, Culture Secretary Jeremy Wright told the Commons on 12 February how the government intended to respond both to those recommendations which they were prepared to progress immediately and others where further consultations were needed. He assured the Commons that the government's response on the entire report would be made later this year.

We must make sure that as a result of this report public money is not used to line the pockets of failed greedy newspaper owners, which will do nothing for good quality journalism and democracy.

## Update

*On 27 January 2020 the government rejected Cairncross's proposals that state funding should be used to support public-interest journalism in the UK, saying that intervention by the government would damage a free press.*

*Culture Secretary, Lady Morgan, (recently appointed to the House of Lords) said: 'It is of vital importance that the press remains free and independent of government, and there are therefore areas where intervention by government would be inappropriate.'*

*The government also rejected proposals to extend charitable status to many struggling local news outlets.*

*You can read the Cairncross report at:*
*https://assets.publishing.service.gov.uk/government/uploads/system/uploads/attachment_data/file/779509/021119_THE_CAIRNCROSS_REVIEW_A_sustainable_future_for_journalism.pdf*

*The government's response to the Cairncross report is at:*
*https://hansard.parliament.uk/commons/2020-01-27/debates/2001276000008/CairncrossReviewGovernmentResponse*

## 51  What sort of media do we want?

### 21 March 2019

**Last Saturday saw the launch of the Media Reform Coalition's (MRC) Media Manifesto 2019 at its Media Democracy Festival in London.**

The well-attended festival was built around the theme of democratising the media, and the various diverse workshops looked at just how this should be done.

The manifesto is built on extensive research and a number of briefing reports from a wide range of specialists and media reform campaigners. It follows in the tradition established by the Campaign for Press and Broadcasting Freedom (now disbanded) which had for many years published a Media Manifesto in advance of general elections to place policy choices for media reform before the public and political parties.

The manifesto is in four parts. The first outlines a framework for achieving media plurality, pointing to the fact that just three companies (News UK, Daily Mail Group and Reach) dominate 83 per cent of the national newspaper market (up from 71 per cent in 2015). It also highlights the threat to media plurality posed by tech giants like Google and Facebook and makes proposals for reform.

The second part sets out ideas for a more democratic, diverse, devolved and independent BBC pointing out that the BBC's independence has been steadily eroded and its programme-making commercialised.

Turning to the need to diversify the workforce adequately, the manifesto points out that ensuring this will require complete transparency about the make-up of the BBC's workforce, and make appropriate recommendations.

Part three sets out urgent steps that a new government must take to restore confidence and trust in a free, accountable and sustainable press. This section includes ideas for a new funding settlement for public interest news (there was extensive discussion on the Cairncross recommendations in one of the workshops) and the need for better privacy for journalists by amending the Investigatory Powers Act 2016 (nicknamed the Snooper's Charter).

The final part 'A Digital Media Policy for the 21st Century' outlines reforms of digital media policies including proposals put forward by Jeremy Corbyn MP in his Alternative McTaggart lecture last year for a new British Digital Corporation. Recommendations to reinforce net neutrality are also outlined.

The festival also saw the launch of the revised edition of the MRC's UK media ownership report.

The Coalition produced its first comprehensive report on media ownership in the UK in 2015. The latest report argues that, then, the concentrated ownership in the UK was 'a significant problem for any modern democracy.' It goes on to say, 'Four years later, we have produced an updated report that suggests that, not only does concentrated ownership persist, but that the problem may be getting worse.'

The report finds that in the area of local news, just five companies (Gannett, JPIMedia, Trinity Mirror, Tindle and Archant) account for 80 per cent of titles (back in 2015, six companies had the same share). Two companies have 46 per cent of all commercial local analogue radio stations and two-thirds of all commercial digital stations. The report goes on to find that the digital landscape is hardly less concentrated:

> Google dominates search while popular apps like Instagram and WhatsApp are owned by Facebook, itself the most popular social media site. New, digital-only news sites have emerged as a significant force since our last report but these are overshadowed by the continuing grip of legacy news and, especially, national newspaper titles.

The MRC hopes that this ownership report will provide information and arguments that will be useful to all who want to campaign for a more pluralistic and trusted media in which a genuine diversity of views, voices and opinions are aired.

Finally, the meeting was urged to promote a model motion through their local parties for the next Labour Party Conference and election manifesto to set out policy objectives to achieve a more democratic, trusted and accountable media.

*More details may be found on the MRC website, including a copy of the updated media ownership report at:*
*https://www.mediareform.org.uk/*
*Questions on the report (including requests for printed copies) and on other aspects of the campaign to MRC at:*
*info@mediareform.org.uk*

## 52 Urgent action needed to support public service broadcasting says Lords committee

*7 November 2019*

**Just hours before Parliament was dissolved at one minute past midnight on 6 November, the House of Lords' Communications and Digital Committee published a report calling for urgent action to safeguard the future of public service broadcasting.**

The report—*Public service broadcasting: as vital as ever*—points to the current threats and calls for urgent measures to safeguard the future of broadcasting as an important part of UK society and democracy.

It warns that public service broadcasters (PSBs) need to be better supported to ensure that they can continue to produce high-quality drama and documentaries that reflect and examine UK culture. In return, the broadcasters need to adapt to ensure that they serve and reflect all audiences.

The committee also raises concerns about the integrity of the licence fee as the guarantor of the BBC's financial independence, describing how it has been undermined by a succession of settlements carried out behind closed doors.

It condemns the decision to hand over responsibility to the BBC for free licences for the over-75s, saying: 'The BBC should not have been offered, or accepted, responsibility for over-75s' licences.'

The committee calls for a new, independent and transparent process for setting the licence fee and recommends the establishment of a new body called the BBC Funding Commission to help set the licence fee.

In its background introduction the report reminds us that:

> twenty years ago, most people relied on five free-to-air terrestrial channels provided by public service broadcasters (PSBs) with a statutory public service remit. The output of commercial broadcasters was available to only a minority of viewers who subscribed to Sky or cable services. Since then choice has increased dramatically. In 1998 the Broadcasters' Audience Research Bureau (an independent body which monitors viewing figures) reported on 57 channels, while in 2018 it reported on 342 (at the time of writing this was the most recent year for which figures were available). Television was generally watched at the time of broadcast—recording on VHS was the exception. The

introduction of technology such as the digital video recorder (such as TiVo) and internet-enabled catch-up services has enabled viewers to watch TV when it suits them. For some, especially many young people, watching so-called 'linear' TV in real-time is now the exception rather than the norm. Viewers also watch content on a range of devices including smartphones, laptops and tablets.

Faced with a revolution in technology, the unprecedented competition from Netflix, Amazon Prime and other subscription video on demand services and subsequent changes in viewing behaviour, the report includes the following recommendations:

**Listed sports events:** The committee recommends a modest increase in the number of listed sports events, which must be shown free to air. This could include The Ashes and The Open Golf Championship.
**TV production:** The UK production sector is a national success story, but it is at risk of reaching full capacity and overheating. The committee recommends changes to High-End TV tax relief and the Apprenticeship Levy, as well as a review of the Terms of Trade between PSBs and independent producers to determine whether they should still apply to larger companies (see para 125–132 of the Report).
**Regulation and funding:** The Government should support PSBs in the new technological environment, and think very carefully before imposing any further regulatory or financial burdens on them. The committee does not support a levy on subscription video on demand services at the moment.

The report's summary sets out 33 recommendations. The report itself has been welcomed by the NUJ. Commenting, General Secretary Michelle Stanistreet said:

This report raises clear alarm bells about the future of public service broadcasting in the UK and the perils it currently faces. Given the current parlous levels of public discourse, and political divisions that exist, quality well-resourced journalism is needed more than ever and public service broadcasting is vital. The NUJ agrees that urgent action is needed to address the challenges public service broadcasting faces and this should be prioritised by the incoming government after the general election.

*Sources*
*Among those giving evidence to the committee were Professor Des Freedman and Dr Tom Mills from the Media Reform Coalition. Their evidence can be found at:*
*http://data.parliament.uk/writtenevidence/committeeevidence.svc /evidencedocument/communications-committee/public-service-broadcasting-in-the-age-of-video-on-demand/oral/101527.html*

BECTU (Prospect) the broadcasting union also gave evidence at: http://data.parliament.uk/writtenevidence/committeeevidence.svc/evidencedocument/communications-committee/public-service-broadcasting-in-the-age-of-video-on-demand/oral/101810.html

The full report is at: https://publications.parliament.uk/pa/ld201920/ldselect/ldcomuni/16/16.pdf

# 53 Election 2019—Future of the Media— what the parties say

## 23 November 2019

**With less than three weeks to go before the general election on 12 December all the main parties have published their election manifestos.**

Below are their proposals on the future of the media, which I have taken from their manifestos (or 'Contract with the People' in the case of the Brexit Party).

**Brexit Party**
Scrap the licence fee by phasing out the BBC licence fee, which is currently £154.50 a year for most people.

**Conservative and Unionist Party**
We recognise the value of free TV licences for over-75s and believe they should be funded by the BBC.

Through the Cultural Investment Fund… we will also support activities, traditions and events that bring communities together. We will support local and regional newspapers, as vital pillars of communities and local democracy, including by extending their business rates relief.

We will champion freedom of expression and tolerance, both in the UK and overseas. To support free speech, we will repeal section 40 of the Crime and Courts Act 2014, which seeks to coerce the press. We will not proceed with the second stage of the Leveson Inquiry.

We will continue our campaigns to promote international media freedom.

**Green Party**
Protect the BBC, reinstate free TV licences for over-75-year-olds and tighten the rules on media ownership so no individual or company owns more than 20 per cent of a media market. To further challenge the control of our media by big tech and unaccountable billionaires, the

Green Party will ensure that a suitable independent regulator is better able to safeguard a healthy plurality of media ownership, to undertake regular plurality reviews and to trigger remedies where necessary.

The recommendations of the 2012 Leveson Report will be implemented, to hold the UK press to high ethical standards.

Support, through new grants, the growth of a wider range of civic-minded local news publishers. Local newspapers in the UK are an important part of our democracy and culture yet many are closing or struggling to survive.

Introduce a Digital Bill of Rights that establishes the UK as a leading voice on standards for the rule of law and democracy in digital spaces and ensure independent regulation of social media providers. This legislation will safeguard elections by responding to the challenges of foreign interference, social media and declining confidence in democracy.

Introduce a public interest defence for breaching the Official Secrets Act, alongside better protection and support for whistle-blowers in the public and private sectors.

## Labour Party

A Labour government will ensure a healthy future for all our public service broadcasters, including BBC Alba and S4C. We will protect free TV licences for over-75s.

A free and fair press is vital to protecting democracy and holding the powerful to account.

We will address misconduct and the unresolved failures of corporate governance raised by the second stage of the abandoned Leveson Inquiry. We will take steps to ensure that Ofcom is better able to safeguard a healthy plurality of media ownership and to put in place clearer rules on who is fit and proper to own or run TV and radio stations. We will take action to address the monopolistic hold the tech giants have on advertising revenues and will support vital local newspapers and media outlets.

We will consult media-sector workers and trade unions to establish an inquiry into the 'fake news' undermining trust in media, democracy and public debate, and on a legal right of public interest defence for journalists.

## Lib Dems

A well-functioning democracy should have a high standard of public debate in which:

- citizens are supported, educated and empowered to distinguish between facts and lies;
- there is a pluralistic media environment where journalists have the resources they need to find the truth and to hold the powerful to account;

- civility in public discourse is protected;
- election procedures and rules are upheld robustly and quickly.

However, these foundations of our democratic way of life are under threat. Liberal Democrats are the only party forward-looking enough to do what it takes to foster high quality public debate. We will:

- mandate the provision of televised leaders' debates in general elections, based on rules produced by Ofcom;
- introduce a Leveson-compliant regulator to be given oversight of both privacy and quality, diversity and choice in both print and online media and proceed with Part Two of the Leveson Inquiry;
- expect the BBC both to provide impartial news and information, and to take a leading role in increasing media literacy and educating all generations in tackling the impact of fake news;
- strengthen and expand the lobbying register and ban MPs from accepting paid lobbying work;
- review the need for any election safeguarding legislation that is needed to respond to emerging challenges of the internet age, such as foreign interference in elections;
- protect the independence of the BBC and set up a BBC Licence Fee Commission, maintain Channel 4 in public ownership and protect the funding and editorial independence of Welsh language broadcasters.

### Plaid Cymru

Plaid Cymru is seeking the devolution of broadcasting so that we can create a level playing field with every other UK nation and give Wales the power to decide its own media and broadcasting policy. In government we will promote a Welsh media that represents the people of Wales and what matters to them.

### Scottish National Party

We continue to believe that responsibility for broadcasting in Scotland should transfer from Westminster to the Scottish Parliament. In the meantime we welcome the creation of a new BBC Scotland TV channel and its associated investment. We will continue to push for greater authority and funding to be moved from BBC network to BBC Scotland. We will also continue to push for a fairer share of the TV licence fee raised in Scotland being spent in Scotland.

We welcome the proposals for the relocation of Channel 4 out with London (sic), and SNP MPs will make a strong case for as many functions of the Channel 4 operation as possible to be based in Scotland.

As the UK government consults on proposals to reduce the requirement for local content on radio, SNP MPs will seek to protect local news and other content provided by local commercial radio stations, recognising the valuable contribution they make to informing and entertaining listeners.

We remain committed to a vibrant, free press and we will work with other parties, in Scotland and at Westminster, to ensure it is supported.

We will make the case for the Scottish Parliament to have the power to decide which sporting events in Scotland are included in the list of those that are free to view in Scotland.

We will demand that the UK government reinstates its funding for Gaelic broadcast.

# 54  Media reform—are the parties up to the challenge?

## 7 December 2019

**The central role the media have played in the general election campaign is undeniable.**

So is the pro-Conservative Party dominance of much of the national press together with its anti-Labour party bias. Social media has offered alternative platforms for the parties and people to get their messages across. Since the last election, we have seen increasing consolidation of media ownership. The latest takeover was announced at the end of November when JPIMedia sold the i newspaper and website for a reported £49.6m to the billionaire Lord Rothermere's Daily Mail and General Trust, which owns the Mail on Sunday and MailOnline. Meanwhile press baron David Montgomery is in talks to buy JPIMedia, which owns dozens of major local British newspapers.

So what new policies do the parties offer to counter these concerns and make our media 'fit for purpose'?

The Conservative Party's manifesto does not say much: the party is generally happy with the status quo and the support it gets from the majority of the press, but what the manifesto says is significant.

On free TV licences for the over-75s, it states that: 'We recognise the value of free TV licences for over-75s and believe they should be funded by the BBC.'

The BBC has said it will continue to provide TV licences to over 75s who claim means-tested pension credit.

On the press: '… we will repeal section 40 of the Crime and Courts Act 2013, which seeks to coerce the press' and: 'We will not proceed with the second stage of the Leveson Inquiry'.

This is not new. After the last election the May government said it would repeal section 40 and scrap Leveson 2, but these proposals were not implemented—the government did not have the numbers to pass the necessary legislation.

Natalie Fenton of the Media Reform Coalition strongly criticises the Section 40 decision. She says:

> Section 40 ... is key to persuading the press to join a recognised regulator through a system of carrots and sticks—if a news publisher joins a recognised regulator then access to low cost arbitration becomes mandatory. This removes the threat of potentially huge losses for both ordinary citizens who may be the victims of illegal journalistic behaviour and for publishers who may be threatened by a wealthy litigant who doesn't like what they have printed.

However, Section 40 has been criticised by a number of press freedom organisations as well as the media owners. Tim Gopsill editor of the CPBF's Free Press, writing on Leveson in its final issue (215, Summer 2018) stated that:

> ... we have ended up with a demure and pointless Press Recognition Panel (PRP) and above all the absurd injustice of Section 40 of the Crime and Courts Act under which the redress that people might attain from a publication would depend on which regulator the offender happens to be affiliated to ...

Index on Censorship describes Section 40 as 'a direct threat to press freedom [which] must be scrapped ...'

Labour has six main pledges, including supporting public service broadcasting and local newspapers and media outlets; action to address the monopolistic hold tech giants have on advertising revenues, and to safeguard a healthy plurality of media ownership.

They also promise to provide free 'full-fibre' broadband for every home and business.

In an article in the Guardian's Society on 3 December ('Labour's broadband plan could radically change young people's life chances') Sandra Leaton Gray points out:

> This manifesto commitment goes well beyond flinging an election freebie at voters largely able to pay for subscriptions themselves. ... speed and access are not the only problems. When young people do access the internet, which is most likely to be through a mobile phone, they see different things: those in deprived areas are bombarded with burger and betting advertisements, while young people in more affluent areas are shown advertisements for university open days and sports equipment. ... Sneaky algorithms assess how far you live from a telephone exchange or mobile phone mast, whether you are accessing the internet by phone, copper or fibre broadband, the geolocation of

your IP address, and even the monetary value and age of the device you are using. ...The way to change this grubby commercial practice is to standardise provision.

The article also reminds us that: 'We see parents in deprived areas paying a small fortune for subscriptions offering a few miserly kilobytes of decrepit and creaking copper broadband ...'

This is happening not only in rural areas, but in urban/city internet cold spots. The proposal aims to bring about high-quality provision for all.

The Liberal Democrats also offer six main pledges including the introduction of a Leveson-compliant regulator and holding Leveson 2, while the Green Party offer four pledges. These include the need to: 'safeguard a healthy plurality of media ownership'.

Both the Scottish and Welsh National parties want devolution of media policy to their parliaments.

All but the Conservative Party have made attempts to address some of the long-standing policy concerns highlighted by media reformers, but we need to go much further if we are to have a media that serves our 21st century democracy.

Urgent reform is needed to reclaim the media in the interest of the public.

*For details of manifesto media policies see:*
*http://thespark.me.uk/?p=1173*

## 55 As Julian Assange edges towards freedom, investigative journalism takes a big hit

*6 January 2021*

**It's been a week of mixed fortunes for WikiLeaks co-founder Julian Assange.**

On Monday (4 January, 2021), many were taken aback by the ruling of district judge Vanessa Baraitser not to allow the US to extradite Julian to stand trial on criminal charges of conspiracy, hacking and violations of the 1917 Espionage Act.

However, on closer reading, it was clear that the judge had rejected all the defence arguments against extradition: the need to protect free speech, that the extradition was politically motivated, and that Julian would not get a fair trial in the US.

It was the appalling state of the US prison system that was the key factor and the 'supermax' prison ADX Colorado, where it is generally accepted Julian would have been sent if sentenced by a US court. This, taken with Julian's mental health history, led her to believe that he would be in danger of taking his own life if he was incarcerated there.

Two days after her ruling against the US extradition came the setback when the same Vanessa Baraitser sitting at Westminster magistrates court rejected his application for bail, saying that Julian '… still has an incentive to abscond from these, as yet unresolved, proceedings. As a matter of fairness the US must be allowed to challenge my decision …'

So Julian will remain in Belmarsh prison in south-east London where he has been held for the past 18 months following his eviction from the Ecuadorian embassy, where he sought asylum for seven years.

Immediately following Monday's judgement, NUJ General Secretary Michelle Stanistreet pointed out the implications of the judge's ruling.

'This decision will be welcomed by all who value journalists' ability to report on national security issues,' she commented. 'However, whilst the outcome is the right one, Judge Vanessa Baraitser's judgement contains much that is troubling. Her basis for dismissing the US's extradition request was the suicide risk that Assange poses in a US penal system that would probably have kept him in near total isolation.'

She added that: 'The judge rejected the defence case that the charges against Assange related to actions identical to those undertaken daily by most investigative journalists. In doing so, she leaves open the door for a future US administration to confect a similar indictment against a journalist.'

These are critical points. Vanessa Baraitser spent some 37 of her 40-minute ruling on Monday dismissing the defence case. In the final three minutes came the decision to deny extradition and the reasons why. So she conceded nothing on most of the key points made by the defence. In summary she agreed on almost all points with the arguments put forward by the US government. As a result, Julian Assange, press freedom, investigative journalism and the right to report all remain at risk.

After the verdict, the following statement was issued by the US Justice Department: 'While we are extremely disappointed in the court's ultimate decision, we are gratified that the United States prevailed on every point of law raised. In particular, the court rejected all of Mr Assange's arguments regarding political motivation, political offence, fair trial, and freedom of speech. We will continue to seek Mr Assange's extradition to the United States.'

That seems to sum up the judgment quite well.

However, the American Civil Liberties Union pointed out in a statement reported in the Guardian on 6 January that the charges against Julian were a direct assault on the US first amendment, which protects freedom of the press and freedom of speech.

Other press freedom organisations have been quick to raise concerns about the judgement.

International Federation of Journalists (IFJ) General Secretary, Anthony Bellanger said:

> The IFJ welcomes the judge's decision not to extradite Assange because of the risk the extradition would pose to his health and well-being. However we are disappointed that the judge appears not to adequately address the threat to media freedom his extradition would have posed in today's ruling.
>
> For years the IFJ and all its affiliates, particularly in the UK, Australia and the USA, have been reminding people that the detention of Julian Assange is contrary to international law and the United Nations Universal Declaration of Human Rights. Furthermore, Julian Assange's health has deteriorated dramatically since his imprisonment in April 2019 and the Covid-19 virus in his prison poses a serious threat to the survival of our colleague, holder of the IFJ International Press Card. It is time for the US to drop its attempts to extradite him.

Reporters without Borders Director of International Campaigns, Rebecca Vincent said: 'We are immensely relieved that Julian Assange will not be extradited to the US. At the same time, we are extremely disappointed that the court failed to take a stand for press freedom and journalistic protections, and we disagree with the judge's assessment that the case was not politically motivated and was not centred on journalism and free speech. This decision leaves the door open for further similar prosecutions and will have a chilling effect on national security reporting around the world if the root issues are not addressed.'

Just how the 'root issues' referred to are addressed is an urgent question. Last summer the Law Commission, a statutory independent body that recommends reforms in England and Wales, called for the creation of a public interest defence for people who leak information in violation of the 1989 Official Secrets Act. The law needed to be 'brought into the 21st century', the Commission said.

This would be a good start but, so far, the government has not acted on the recommendation.

Julian's defence team also need to challenge the judge's rejection of their case against extradition, which could, if adopted into law, create a dangerous precedent. This they should do as part of the appeal process of which the US authorities have already given notice.

Meanwhile it's worth remembering that in February 2018 the computer scientist and alleged computer hacker Lauri Love won his High Court appeal against extradition to the US. Appeal judges said extradition would be 'oppressive by reason of his physical and mental condition' after he was arrested on suspicion of hacking into FBI, US Central Bank and NASA systems. His supporters warned if he was extradited there was a 'high risk' Mr Love would kill himself.

With the change of government in the US only days away, it is by no means clear if the Biden administration will take up Julian Assange's prosecution.

The US prosecutor seeking to put Julian on trial in the US has said he was uncertain whether Joe Biden's incoming administration will continue to seek the extradition.

The Guardian reported on 5 January that Zachary Terwilliger, who was appointed by Donald Trump, made the following comments to the US NPR News as he was stepping down as the US attorney for the Eastern District of Virginia (where the case would be heard):

'It will be very interesting to see what happens with this case. There'll be some decisions to be made. Some of this does come down to resources and where you're going to focus your energies.'

Be that as it may, here in the UK we need to keep the pressure up for Julian's release, the US charges to be dropped and the right to report strengthened in the light of the judge's ruling.

There is also the matter of Julian and his family's future. He is an Australian citizen and if the US fails in their bid to extradite him I'm sure the US would love to see him deported from the UK at some time in the future.

That would mean sending him back to Australia, which would allow the US to again start proceedings to extradite him: the Extradition (United States of America) Regulations enables Australia to receive extradition requests from the US!

So what will the UK government do if Julian finally wins his legal case?

Farfetched? You never can be sure, except to say that the struggle is far from over. And if the Biden administration does appeal the decision not to extradite him, the case could drag on into the summer with Julian incarcerated in Belmarsh.

# Mordechai Vanunu

## 56  10 years on and still not free
### 3 April 2013

In the late summer of 1986 Mordechai Vanunu, an Israeli citizen who had been employed at the Dimona Nuclear Power Plant in the Negev Desert, gave evidence to the London Sunday Times newspaper that Israel was developing nuclear weapons. It was an act of conscience and he wanted the World to know. While in London he was lured by a Mossad agent to Italy where in Rome on 30 September he was drugged, kidnapped and transported to Israel to stand trial. In the Jerusalem District Court he was convicted of treason and sentenced to 18 years in Askelon prison. He spent the first eleven and a half years in solitary confinement.

On his release on 21 April 2004, which I witnessed as part of an international delegation and covered in my first book *On the record*, he was subjected to severe restrictions based on legislation in Palestine dating back to the 1945 British Emergency Mandate laws.

He moved to East Jerusalem where he lived for six years. Then in September 2010 he moved to Tel Aviv. He subsequently moved to East Jerusalem. In May 2011, following the passing of a new law which revoked the citizenship of anyone convicted of espionage or treason, Mordechai called on the authorities to revoke his citizenship and be allowed to leave Israel. Wikipedia reported that on 1 May 2012, Vanunu deactivated his Facebook and Twitter accounts after he learnt that the Israeli government was monitoring them.

On 6 June 2012, the High Court of Justice denied Vanunu's petition to renounce his Israeli citizenship. In response Vanunu said, "I want them to revoke my citizenship so that I can begin my life." Nevertheless, Vanunu continued to be subject to draconian restrictions and judicial harassment.

Then on 10 May 2016 the Guardian reported that twelve years after his release, Vanunu, was facing charges of violating the terms of his original release. His alleged crime was that in 2013 he met two US nationals at a hotel in East Jerusalem, without permission. He was also accused of moving to a different flat in his apartment building in

2014, and failing to inform the police about it. And, in 2015, he gave an interview to Channel 2 television in which, according to the indictment served at Jerusalem magistrate's court, he gave the interviewer 'classified information that was cut out by censors'. On 18 January 2017, he was convicted on one count of meeting with foreigners.

He is still anxious to leave Israel, but is barred from emigrating on the grounds that he still poses a threat to national security! In the 2015 interview, he said he no longer had any secrets and just wanted to join his wife in Norway, Kristin Joachimsen (a theology professor, whom he married at a Lutheran church in Jerusalem in May).

Vanunu has of course been here before when in 2010 he was jailed for 11 weeks for breaking the terms of his release by meeting a foreigner. Subsequently, he appealed against the restrictions placed on him, including the state's refusal to allow him to leave the country. The appeal was rejected.

Fast forward to last year—little has changed. On 2 June 2019, Vanunu reported at his Facebook Wall, 'that for the 16th year, after 18 years behind bars' Israel renewed the restrictions against Vanunu 'not to meet foreigners, not leave the country'. On 3 December 2019, Israel's Supreme Court dismissed Vanunu's latest petition seeking to end the restraining orders against 'his freedom' and 'privacy' citing 'a concern about the probability of closeness to the certainty that if the restrictions imposed on Vanunu are removed, he will act to publish this [relevant confidential] information.'

On 1 June 2020, Vanunu reported on Twitter: 'They renew all the restrictions for one more year, from June 2020 to June 2021...I will continue to post every month'.

For Vanunu the struggle continues. He has no intention of ever giving up. He deserves our solidarity.

# Durham Miners' Gala

## 57  Banners held high

### 15 July 2015

**This year marks the 30th anniversary of the defeat of the great miners' strike (1984—5). The weekend marked the 131st Durham Miners' Gala (the 'Big Meeting') attended by over 150,000.**

The night before the main event on Saturday 11 July a meeting, organised by the Orgreave Truth and Justice Campaign (OTJC) was held at the miners' HQ in Red Hill, Durham to discuss the latest developments in the campaign to get justice for the Orgreave miners and supporters.

The meeting was opened by Granville Williams from the campaign, who reminded us that, only the day before, Thoresby colliery in Nottingham had shut down with the loss of more than 300 jobs.

This came less than two weeks after the shock closure of Hatfield colliery in South Yorkshire at the end of last month, leaving just one deep coal mine still working in Britain, in Kellingley in West Yorkshire. Taken together, the closed mines will leave underground millions of tonnes of high quality coal which campaigners believe could have been burned using the Carbon Capture and Storage system (CCS). Instead, coal will be imported from abroad. Granville announced that a campaign has been launched by activists at Hatfield to preserve the colliery's pit-head equipment as a fitting memorial to the industry and those who worked in it.

Barbara Jackson, OTJC secretary, updated the meeting on developments since the Independent Police Complaints Commission (IPCC) had announced a few weeks ago that, after two and a half years' 'scoping exercise', they had decided that no independent inquiry would take place into the conduct of the South Yorkshire Police on the day of the mass picket and during the subsequent court cases against 95 miners. Those cases collapsed, resulting in the police paying £425,000 in compensation to 39 miners.

The reason given for not carrying out an inquiry was the length of time that had elapsed since the event (1984). The campaign considered this to be unacceptable, especially in the light of the decision to hold new inquests into the deaths of 96 people at the FA Cup semi-final at Hillsborough (four years after the events of Orgreave).

Barbara told the meeting that they were due to meet Home Secretary Theresa May to put the case for a public inquiry.

Next day, the Big Meeting witnessed its biggest turnout for years. The mood of the participants was positive, the mood of the platform speakers defiant in the wake of the election of the Tory government in May. Trade union leaders Matt Wrack (FBU), Tosh McDonald (ASLEF president and at first glance a Richard Branson look-alike, who 'hated Margaret Thatcher with a passion'), General Secretary of the teachers' union NASUWT, Chris Keates, and Unite leader Len McCluskey were united in their opposition to the government's determination—reinforced by their recent budget with £12 billion in cuts—to destroy the welfare state as we know it. They called for united resistance.

The campaign for a new Labour leader and deputy took central stage at the rally. The organisers had invited Jeremy Corbyn to the meeting and deputy candidate Tom Watson (who spoke at the 2012 Gala).

In a well-received speech, Jeremy thanked the organisers for inviting him to speak, saying that it was 'one of the greatest honours of my life'. He called for a society of full employment, decency, and human rights, and one that abolished poverty.

'It can be done,' he said.

His eight-minute speech went down well and his campaign stall did a roaring trade in tee-shirts, leaflets and stickers.

Also speaking in support of Jeremy was the socialist columnist Owen Jones. It was the second time he had been on the platform and he thrilled the audience with a wide-ranging speech, which started by referring to his grandfather, a railway worker, who struck in solidarity with the miners in 1926. He went on to praise the women who took part in the 1984/85 strike, referring to them as the 'real iron ladies'.

Jones criticised the right-wing press for their constant attacks on the trade union links with the Labour Party—and that party's feeble response, saying that Labour should be proud of the support it gets from workers, unlike the Tories who are funded by bankers, hedge funds and loan sharks, the very people that plunged the country into crisis in 2008.

The official Labour opposition had gone AWOL, he said—we were the official opposition now. He reminded us that the rights we had won over the centuries had been won from below: 'We stand on the shoulders of giants.'

His final call was for unity in the struggles ahead. 'Stand together, fight together, and together we can win these battles together,' he concluded.

All in all an inspirational day—and the weather was good!

*For more information about the OTJC and the background go to: http://otjc.org.uk/*

*You can see Jeremy's speech on YouTube at: https://www.youtube.com/watch?v=MpKhRURuXSs*

*Owen's is at: https://www.youtube.com/watch?v=CIG1czpgooQ*

## 58  Tens of thousands celebrate the 135th Durham Miners' Gala—where campaigners highlight the proposed rendition of Julian Assange to the US

*27 July 2019*

**Saturday 13 July saw a massive turnout at the 135th Big Meeting organised by the Durham Miners' Association (DMA), now in its 150th year.**

The organisers claim that the Gala is the largest celebration of community and working class culture in the world and it is a tribute to the DMA, who have revived the celebrations in recent years, giving it stronger community, national and international involvements.

Despite the brutal shutting down of the UK's mining industry following the 1984/85 miners' strike and the devastation of their communities which threatened the very future of the DMA, the Big Meeting goes from strength to strength.

Much of this is due to the setting up in 2015 of Marras, the Friends of Durham Miners' Gala.

The Friends was set up by the Durham Miners' Association, together with several major trade unions, to secure the long-term future of the Gala. They aim to bring together individuals and groups to support the Gala financially, and create a fund to cover its running costs, as well as to support various community banner groups. By working together they aim to make sure that the principles carried forward over the Gala's long history are upheld for generations to come.[1]

Despite Saturday's mid-morning rain, the crowds, many of whom had marched behind their local banners, greeted the platform speakers with enthusiasm—none more so than local MP Laura Pidcock, who was cheered to the overcast skies. She spoke strongly against the prospect of a Johnson-led government which she saw as continuing Margaret Thatcher's neo-liberal economic free market policies. 'Disillusion and disappointment haunt our communities,' she said, adding that exploitation is commonplace, yet invisible.

Other women platform speakers were Shami Chakrabarti, Labour's shadow Attorney General (who spoke at the Dave Hopper Memorial Lecture the evening before the Gala), and Rebecca Long-Bailey, bringing a better gender balance to the platform than in previous years. The crowd also heard from other platform speakers including Len McCluskey, head of Unite, Dave Ward head of the Communications Workers Union and Dave Prentis of UNISON.

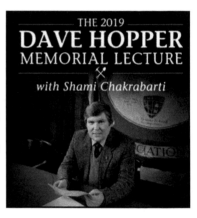

But it was left to Labour's leader, Jeremy Corbyn, to set out the party's radical alternative vision for the future, seeking to heal the divisions brought about by the 2016 referendum. He reassured listeners that anti-semitism and racism would not be tolerated. As the rain cleared, the Labour leader said that he wanted to lead a Labour government that would transform society and offer real hope to the next generation.

The sun came out and the appreciative crowd gave him an enthusiastic send-off, especially following his commitment that a future Labour government would investigate police violence against the miners during the 1984/85 strike including that which took place at Orgreave in South Yorkshire.

Another important feature of the Gala is the presence of dozens of trade union, community, political and campaigning organisations promoting their campaigns. This year there was a stall in support of the campaign to stop the deportation of the WikiLeaks founder and journalist Julian Assange to the United States. It was organised by the Socialist Equality Party, who also interviewed me about the case.[2]

Julian faces extradition proceedings following a decision last month by the then Home Secretary Sajid Javid (now Chancellor of the Exchequer) to agree to extradition proceeding in the British courts. The decision came a few days after an attempt to extradite him to Sweden suffered a setback, when a court in Uppsala said he did not need to be detained. According to press reports, the ruling by the district court prevents Swedish prosecutors from immediately applying for an extradition warrant for Assange to face an allegation of rape dating back to 2010, which he denies.

Incidentally, if you want to read a very thorough account of the attempts by the Swedish authorities to secure Julian's extradition, you can do no better than turn to the account given by Geoffrey Robinson QC in his excellent book *Rather His Own Man: In Court with Tyrants, Tarts and Troublemakers* (Biteback Publishing, 2018, Chapter 14: 'Assange in Ecuador'). Geoffrey describes in great detail how the US had been hurt by a 'pesky Australian', 'so they targeted him by grand jury proceedings and the military took out its anger on young Chelsea Manning, treating her abominably in prison, until Hilary Clinton's press spokesman, P.J. Crowley, resigned in protest...' (in March 2011).

Geoffrey Robinson, a world-famous human rights lawyer, defended Julian against extradition proceedings in the United Kingdom some nine years ago. Chelsea Manning is now in prison for a second time for refusing to testify to a US federal grand jury investigating WikiLeaks. She continues to object to the secrecy of the grand jury process and now faces a fine of $500 for every day she refuses to testify.

The threats to both Julian and Chelsea are serious. Julian faces a maximum sentence of 175 years in prison in the US if convicted of all the charges against him, which is why a strong world-wide campaign is urgently needed.

After the WikiLeaks founder was forcibly removed from the Ecuadorian embassy in London and arrested earlier this year, NUJ Assistant General Secretary Seamus Dooley said:

> The NUJ is shocked and concerned by the actions of the authorities today in relation to Julian Assange. His lawyer has confirmed he has been arrested not just for breach of bail conditions, but also in relation to a US extradition request. The UK should not be acting on behalf of the Trump administration in this case. The NUJ recognises the inherent link between and importance of leaked confidential documents and journalism reporting in the public interest. It should be remembered

that in April 2010 WikiLeaks released *Collateral Murder*, a video showing a 2007 US Apache helicopter attack upon individuals in Baghdad: more than 23 people were killed including two Reuters journalists. The manner in which Assange is treated will be of great significance to the practice of journalism.

At last month's International Federation of Journalists' (IFJ) congress in Tunisia, the NUJ supported an emergency motion highlighting the severe dangers to journalism posed by the recent indictments filed by the US government against Julian Assange. Congress called for this to be resisted by the governments of the UK and Australia, highlighting how the decision to prosecute, for the receipt and publication of information in the public interest, is clearly at odds with previous decisions of the US Supreme Court to protect First Amendment rights.

These are solid foundations to strengthen the international campaign to get the charges dropped against Julian and strike a blow for press freedom and the right to report in the public interest.

In the meantime the plight of Chelsea Manning must not be forgotten. Let us do our best to make sure both she and Julian Assange are free by the time the Gala meets next year.

As the campaigning journalist and film-maker John Pilger says, 'Chelsea Manning and Julian Assange are as brave and principled as any who struggled for historic rights of freedom for all.'

*1. You can find out more about the Gala and join the Friends by going to: https://www.friendsofdurhamminersgala.org/join_us*

*2. Interview with the Socialist Equality Party: https://www.wsws.org/en/articles/2019/07/15/durh-j15.html*

# Election 2019

## 59  The Tory manifesto—an Executive 'power grab'—we have been warned

*26 November 2019*

**If elected on 12 December, will a new Tory government unleash an attack on some of the democratic traditions we have taken for granted for many years?**

After all, during the last parliament there were frequent attacks on MPs' attempts to hold the government to account over Brexit because, as representatives of the people, they wanted to have a final say on the proposed withdrawal deal and on any attempt to take 'no deal' off the table. A case of the Commons 'taking back control' you might say.

The Commons, elected only two years earlier, reflected the close division in the UK over leaving the EU, so it was no surprise after the election when the government, having failed to seek a cross-party approach to leaving, acted in the way they did. But it was not just the Commons that sought to 'take back control', to exercise parliamentary sovereignty, there were other forces—including the courts.

That's not the way the right-wing press saw it over the past three years. Accusations of 'Enemies of the People' and 'The House of Fools' (Daily Mail), 'EU Dirty Rats' (Sun) and 'Parliament surrenders to the EU' (Daily Express) were flung at those who had the nerve to hold the government to account.

In September 2017, the Supreme Court ruled in favour of giving MPs a say over triggering Article 50—the legal mechanism taking the UK out of the EU.

The May government did not want parliament to have such a say. Two years later, the campaigner Gina Miller was back in court, this time over the decision of Prime Minister Johnson to recommend the Queen to suspend parliament. The Supreme Court found in her favour, ruling that the decision to suspend parliament was unlawful.

Meanwhile Boris Johnson went on record as describing parliament as a 'nuisance' and a threat to his policy of taking Britain out of the EU by his deadline of 31 October.

Fast forward to the publication of the Conservative manifesto for the 2019 general election, page 48, which reads:

> After Brexit we also need to look at the broader aspects of our constitution: the relationship between the government, parliament and the courts; the functioning of the Royal prerogative; the role of the House of Lords; and access to justice for ordinary people. The ability of our security services to defend us against terrorism and organised crime is critical. We will update the Human Rights Act and administrative law to ensure that there is a proper balance between the rights of individuals, our vital national security and effective government.

Fair enough? Not according to Sean O'Grady, writing in the online Independent on 25 November.

He warns: 'I think they're going to scrap the remaining practical rights and prerogatives of the House of Commons in an act of spite.'

Referring to the parliamentary procedures used by the Commons to take control over the order of business of the house and making ministers accountable for their actions he warns that:

> ... [a] Johnson administration, if elected, is going to stop all that malarkey. They will also—it is more or less explicit—interfere in the judiciary and restrict the powers of the Supreme Court to rule on issues such as the prorogation of parliament. There has been talk—not in this manifesto admittedly—of making the judges politically accountable, by being ratified via hearings by parliament, in the way they are in the United States. They have not forgiven Lady Hale and her colleagues for their ruling that the suspension of parliament in the autumn was unlawful, null and void. Neither would I be surprised if they pack the Lords with new and obedient Tory peers.

The manifesto also says that:

> The failure of Parliament to deliver Brexit—the way so many MPs have devoted themselves to thwarting the democratic decision of the British people in the 2016 referendum—has opened up a destabilising and potentially extremely damaging rift between politicians and people. If the Brexit chaos continues, with a second referendum and a second Scottish referendum too, they will lose faith even further.

And how will these changes be brought about? The manifesto continues:

> In our first year we will set up a Constitution, Democracy & Rights Commission that will examine these issues in depth, and come up with proposals to restore trust in our institutions and in how our democracy operates.

The problems go wider than this. No doubt the commission would undertake a public consultation, which it would consider, but it would be foolish to deny serious public concerns about parliament's disconnection with many sections of the public and its failure to speak up for many of those it represents. The expenses scandal that erupted over ten years ago and shook the political system to its foundation lives long in the public memory. And as Chris McLaughlin, Tribune's editor-at-large, pointed out in its summer edition:

> Nine years ago, a two-year inquiry by a specially appointed speaker's conference on Parliamentary Representation concluded that: 'at present few people think that MPs understand, or share, the life experiences of the people they represent'.

That report lamented the:

> under-representation of groups, such as women, ethnic minorities, LGBT communities, as well as the decline in people voting in elections...

If they do form a government after 12 December, will the Tories' new commission take seriously and review the recommendations made in 2010 by the Speaker's Conference? Or will they use it to strengthen the powers of the executive over parliament, and maybe even the courts, and further curtail our civil liberties in the interests of 'effective government'?

After all, it was only in April that the Hansard Society's audit of political engagement reported that the UK public was increasingly disenchanted with MPs and government, and ever more willing to welcome the idea of authoritarian leaders who would ignore parliament.

Almost three-quarters of those asked said the system of governance needed significant improvement, and other attitudes emerged that 'challenge core tenets of our democracy', the audit's authors stated.

The study, compiled annually by the democracy charity, found that when people were asked whether 'Britain needs a strong ruler willing to break the rules', 54 per cent agreed and only 23 per cent said no.

These findings, taken with Johnson's record and the proposals set out in the Conservative manifesto, should sound alarm bells.

# History

## 60 Under the Pennines and back in time
*16 September 2014*

**Last Saturday was a real highlight for me. I travelled the three miles on the Huddersfield Narrow Canal between Marsden in West Yorkshire and Diggle in Greater Manchester.**

What's so special about that?

It's all underground—in the longest canal tunnel in Britain and the third longest in the world. The longest, closed in 1963, is 'Le Rove', which runs for 7120 metres between Marseilles and the Rhone. The second, at 5677m, is 'Le Grand Souterain' near Riqueval north-east of Paris and is still open and in use. The Standedge Tunnel is a close third at 5210m (3.23 miles).

I got to know about Standedge and the Huddersfield canal in the 1980s when I first visited the area. Then the canal, which runs from Huddersfield to Ashton-under-Lyne, was in need of serious renovation. Now, thanks to the vision and hard work of many volunteers, the work has been done, but pride of place goes to those who campaigned and finally reopened the tunnel on 1 May 2001.

Standedge Tunnel, the longest canal tunnel in the Britain

But how we got here is really interesting.

Work first began on the Narrow Canal in 1794. It was an ambitious plan to tunnel for some three miles under the Pennines at Standedge, with nothing more than gunpowder, picks and shovels and, of course, the navvies, who took all the risks.

According to our guides on the trip, they started work at both ends with a target of five years to completion (1799). But progress was slow, and those in charge lacked experience. So it was Thomas Telford who rode up to rescue the project. Digging, we were told, had been taking place at both ends, and also, I later found out, from the bottom of the airshafts (through which spoil was hoisted up and onto the moor, where some can still be seen today). It was discovered (nobody quite knows how) that the tunnels would not meet in the middle—they were some 37 feet out, so a number of bends were added to correct the problem.

The tunnel finally opened in 1811, 17 years after the work had begun, at a cost of £123,804. Our guide told us that the cost in human life was great. Fifty navvies were killed while actually digging the tunnel, but any worker who died of his injuries outside the tunnel (having been rescued and brought out into the open) was not counted, and the total numbers of injuries do not seem to have been recorded either.

As we discovered on our two-and-a-quarter-hour trip in our specially adapted craft, the tunnel is very narrow in most places and, to save money on the original construction, no towpath was provided. As the guide explained, the horses we decoupled at the entrances and trekked over the hill to the other side, while the boatmen had to 'leg it' through the tunnel.

As we saw from a very old picture on the craft that took us through, this was done by lying on boards at the front of the boat and walking along the roof or walls of the tunnel. Depending on the load being carried, this could take up to four hours (more when it was first opened), so very soon after the tunnel was opened, official or professional 'leggers' were introduced to speed up the operation. Every 50 yards there is a marker on the roof telling you how far you have gone. This was the only guide to how far you had travelled, as you can't see straight through the tunnel to the light at the other end because of the bends.

As with many canals, early profits and prosperity were brought to an end with the coming of the railways and the canal and tunnel were subsequently bought by the Huddersfield and Manchester Railway Company, whose railway lines and tunnels followed a similar route to the canal. Of course the canal was key in the construction of the new railway and tunnels, but thereafter it fell into decline and was officially closed in 1944, commercial traffic having ceased some 20 years earlier.

Although basic maintenance within the tunnel was carried out in the 1950s and 60s, its state deteriorated, with parts of the roof collapsing, making any journey impossible.

My early memory some 30 years ago was of sealed entrances and little sign of activity. However, a campaign for restoration for the Narrow Canal was underway, but the tunnel was going to be a major operation.

By the late 1990s, funding had been secured and work got underway. The tunnel was, by all accounts, not a pretty sight. Some parts were silted up to six feet deep. Sections of the roof had collapsed and others were unstable.

Access for vehicles and machinery was difficult as most of the tunnel measured only around seven feet wide. Hopes to re-open the tunnel during the millennium remained just that: restoration had become a major operation with 10,000 tons of silt and 3,000 tons of fallen rock being removed. Sections of the tunnel had to be lined with concrete.

But, on May Day 2001, the tunnel was opened to traffic once again, at a cost of more than £5m. Unlike the 1811 opening, I don't believe the event was marked with church bells and a band playing 'Rule Britannia'.

However, it meant the entire length of the canal from Huddersfield to Ashton-under-Lyne, some 20 miles, was open for business once again.

But it is not commercial business this time. Narrow boats serving tourism now gently run up and down the canal, which has a total of 74 locks and connects with the Ashton Canal and the Huddersfield Broad Canal.

To find out more visit:
*http://www.penninewaterways.co.uk/huddersfield/* or go to the Standedge Visitor Centre near Marsden and don't miss the Tunnel End Cottages, which have been regenerated into the very pleasing Watersedge café.

And for the journey of a lifetime, book yourself onto the 'tunnel experience'. Hard hats are provided and the guides live and breathe the canal and tunnel. As one explained to us, it is the best job he has ever had.

# 61  Angela's story—a unique life well remembered

## 28 January 2016

**This week, I went to a meeting organised by the London Socialist Historians Group to hear Rosie MacGregor, a long-standing Nalgo and UNISON colleague, speak about her recently published book on the life of Angela Gradwell Tuckett.**

Rosie had told me about the book when we met by chance at last November's demonstration and parliamentary lobby against the government's Trade Union Bill.

Angela was born in Bristol in 1906 into a well-off, politically aware family, which had a strong Quaker influence. She was a feminist, the first woman solicitor in Bristol (she worked for her father's firm), peace campaigner, qualified pilot, journalist and author and folk musician.

She was also a keen hockey player who represented England and was a member of the national team that played in a tournament in Germany in 1935. Rosie explains that the team 'had to pass through a cordon of Hitler youth all giving the Nazi salute as they entered the stadium.'

Obviously (unlike the rest of the team) Angela did not return their salute. This got her into trouble with the authorities (from both countries) and she was never again selected to play for England.

A few years earlier, in 1931, after seeing the plight of hunger marchers, she had joined the Communist Party and, later, became head of the Legal Department of the National Council for Civil Liberties (now Liberty). She then joined the staff of the Daily Worker (now the Morning Star) before moving to Labour Monthly.

A loyal and unquestioning member of the Communist Party, she moved to Swindon in 1962 when she married her second husband, Ike Gradwell, who was also a member of the Communist Party.

She died in Swindon in 1994.

Rosie's excellent, honest and well-researched account brings Angela to life (warts and all) and is a great tribute to a campaigner who hated injustice and wanted to build a better world based on socialist principles.

*Publication details:* Angela Remembered: The Life of Angela Gradwell Tuckett *by Rosie MacGregor is published by WaterMarx, on behalf of the White Horse (Wiltshire) Trades Council, 2015, ISBN 978-0-9570726-3-3, price £7.50.*

## 62  Sensational election result in Walthamstow

### 10 February 2016

**How was it that Sam Woods, a former hewer (miner) from Wigan and a complete outsider, managed to win the formerly Tory seat of Walthamstow at a by-election in 1897?**

I found the answer in an article written by John Shepherd, a principal lecturer at Cambridge College of Arts and Technology, in the 1987 edition of the Essex Journal.

Woods won the seat for the small group of working class MPs known as Lib-Labs who represented working class and labour interests, but were politically Liberals.

In 1897 the Essex county constituencies of Romford and Walthamstow had the two largest electorates in the country. Voting rights were very limited and the South Western Division had 19,846 male voters out of a population of some 150,000. It was a vast constituency, taking in Walthamstow, Leyton, Leytonstone, Harrow Green and Woodford.

The area had grown rapidly. Before 1850 there were fewer than 5,000 people in the rural parish of Walthamstow. Between 1873 and 1891 the population leaped from 11,092 to 95,131—mainly due to the coming of the railway, which turned the area into a new, mainly working-class suburb which included skilled artisans and clerks, many of whom worked in the City.

The socialist William Morris, who was born in Walthamstow, described it in 1883 as 'a pleasant place enough, but now terribly cocknified and choked up by the jerrybuilder'.

His description seems to exclude my home (for the last 31 years) in Walthamstow 'village', which was built in 1862.

At the time, the Liberal Party found it difficult to get wealthy members to fight elections in the constituency. Elections were, after all, an expensive business. A prominent local Liberal bigwig wrote to Herbert Gladstone (Home Secretary from 1905 to 1910 and youngest son of the 19th century Prime Minister, William Ewart Gladstone) to say that: 'I am afraid this division is a forlorn hope. I shall do what I can for the candidate they choose though I should not stand myself.'

According to Shepherd, the vacancy in 1897 was brought about by the appointment of the sitting Tory MP, E.W. Byrne QC, to the Chancery Division of the High Court. The local Tories quickly selected Thomas Dewar, a wealthy director of Dewar's Whisky, as their man.

After a lot of delay, Sam Woods, secretary of the parliamentary committee of the TUC was persuaded to stand and funds (nearly £1,400) were made available.

Obviously, Woods was not from the middle-class elite which dominated many Liberal associations but, recognising the changing nature of the constituency, he was endorsed by the party and one Herbert (later Viscount) Samuel organised the local campaign.

According to election material distributed at the time, Sam Woods had entered the mines aged seven and had worked at every mining occupation for 20 years. From humble beginnings he became a labour leader with strong Baptist and temperance beliefs—a contrast to his rival the whisky (later) baron, Dewar.

Sam was a radical who favoured a broad Lib-Lab alliance. His programme reflected his radicalism:

> I strongly favour such democratic proposals as the abolition of the power of the House of Lords to veto legislation, the payment of MPs, one man one vote, a thorough Registration reform and the control by the Irish people of their own domestic affairs. I also heartily support the taxation of Ground values, a radical reform of the Land Laws as affecting both urban and rural land, the establishment of a complete system of secondary education open to all classes and any measures which would improve the housing of the people.

The campaign was vigorous and, according to Shepherd, three days before the poll, Woods spoke at 13 meetings that day.

Election day, Wednesday, 3 February, had been preceded by heavy snow the night before. The Liberal camp was not optimistic about a victory, but a 64 per cent turnout resulted in a Lib-Lab majority of 279 (the previous general election result gave the Tories a majority of 2,353).

Although he had united progressives in Walthamstow, Sam was defeated in the 1900 general election (known as the Khaki Election, because the result was believed to have been influenced by the supposed end of the Boer War) and retired a few years later.

Although he was in effect Labour's first MP for Walthamstow, the party did not contest a parliamentary election in Walthamstow until after the First World War.

In 1922 Valetine la Touche McEntree was elected MP for Labour and, in 1950, the constituency elected one Clement Attlee as its MP.

The rest, as they say, is history.

## 63 *An Inspector Calls*

### *3 August 2020*

**The other week I watched for the second time the 2015 TV film *An Inspector Calls*. It is based on a play by J. B. Priestley that revolves around the apparent suicide of a young woman called Eva Smith.**

As was the case when I first saw it, I found it gripping from beginning to end—and that's not just because it was filmed in Yorkshire and featured one of my favourite locations, Salt's Mill in Saltaire Village, near Bradford.

It is set in 1912, when the unsuspecting and very wealthy Birling family is visited by a mysterious Inspector Goole.

The family is headed by pompous factory owner, Arthur Birling, who is hoping to get a knighthood. He and his snobbish wife Sybil and young son Eric are celebrating the engagement of daughter Sheila to eligible Gerald Croft (rich, privileged and a member of the aristocracy) when the 'Inspector' calls.

The Inspector reveals that a girl called Eva Smith has taken her own life by drinking disinfectant. The family are horrified, but don't understand why the Inspector has called to see them.

What follows is a tense and uncomfortable investigation by an all-knowing Inspector through which the family discover that they are all in fact caught up in this woman's death. This the Inspector does by showing that each had, in their own way, contributed to her tragic end. Eva had been dismissed from work at the local textile factory owned by Arthur Birling: he had sacked her for having organised a strike which the workers lost. In the young men's cases, both had had sexual relationships with her, and then abandoned her.

I won't tell you how it ends as I really recommend that you view it.

The play was first performed in the Soviet Union in 1945 and at the New Theatre in Covent Garden in London the following year. The theatre was renamed the Gillian Lynne Theatre in 2018 after the English actress, ballerina, choreographer, dancer, and director who died later that year.

As it is set in 1912, it means that the characters have no knowledge of the world-shattering events that took place over the following 30 and more years. Priestley uses this to make important points about society and responsibility.

Which brings me to Priestley himself. I first saw the play in the early 1960s performed by the St Nicholas Players, an amateur group of players drawn from the local parish church in Sutton, Surrey, but I did not understand its political significance, nor the politics of the Yorkshire playwright, who was also a novelist, screenwriter, broadcaster and social commentator.

Priestley was a founding member of the Campaign for Nuclear Disarmament (CND) in 1958. Well before then, in 1942, he co-founded the Common Wealth, of which more later. The political content of his wartime broadcasts and his hopes of a new and different Britain after the war influenced the politics of the period and is said to have helped the Labour Party achieve its stunning landslide victory over Churchill and the Conservative Party in the 1945 summer general election.

Interestingly 'JB' was named on George Orwell's March 1949 list of people which he drew up for the Information Research Department (IRD), a propaganda unit at the Foreign Office set up by the Labour Government. Orwell considered or suspected people on it to have pro-communist leanings and therefore to be unsuitable to write for the department whose mission it was to counter Soviet propaganda and infiltration. Although the existence of the department was supposed to be a secret, the USSR knew all about it as the Soviet agent Guy Burgess had been posted to IRD for two months in 1948 before being sacked for being 'dirty, drunk and idle.'

The Common Wealth movement was a left social democratic organisation based on three principles: Common Ownership, Morality in Politics and Vital Democracy. It disagreed with the electoral pact established between the main political parties in the wartime coalition and began sponsoring independent candidates in by-elections. It had a number of successes including winning a seat in Skipton, not far from my home in Settle, North Yorkshire.

In the 1945 general election voters deserted the movement in favour of Labour and they only hung on to Chelmsford in Essex, where the seat was not contested by Labour. The following year the organisation split, with the majority joining the Labour Party. The organisation carried on as a pressure group, a shadow of its former self, and in 1992 members and supporters met in London for a 50th anniversary lunch. A year later the organisation wound up at a meeting in Cheltenham.

JB had a dark side. Despite being a progressive and a socialist, his attitude to the Irish was racist, associating them with ignorance, dirt and drunkenness, a view not uncommon at the time, but unacceptable in a person who believed in socialism, tolerance and decency.

Priestley died of pneumonia on 14 August 1984 and is buried in St Michael and All Angels' Church in Hubberholme in North Yorkshire.

# Plymouth Argyle FC

## 64  To be a Pilgrim!
### *6 June 2018/August 2020*

**For almost as long as I can remember I have been a supporter of Plymouth Argyle FC, popularly known as 'The Pilgrims'.**

Now, as the football season has just come to an end, it's time for reflection. Why Plymouth you may ask? Well, it dates back to my childhood. My father was born in Newton Abbot in Devonshire, some 30 miles from Plymouth. His father was a carpenter working in the dockyards in the city, and despite there being two other Devonshire teams, Exeter and Torquay (which were a lot nearer) we always followed the fortunes of Argyle.

As I remember, Plymouth was usually regarded as the top team in the county and rivalry between the three clubs was legendary, especially between the two cities. I'm not quite in that league, being an outsider and I've always had a soft spot for the other two Devonshire clubs, but my first loyalty was and is to 'The Pilgrims'.

The first time I saw Argyle was when I travelled up on my motorbike (a James 150cc) from the family home in Sutton, in Surrey, (some 14 miles from central London) to watch them play Leyton Orient in East London in an evening fixture on Tuesday 3 September 1963. It was a League Division 2 (now called The Championship) game. Plymouth played in a very smart continental-looking strip of white, green and black and, despite the fashionable turnout, they lost 1—0.

The next game I recall was Argyle's home game against Southampton on 7 May 1966 in the penultimate match of the season (the World Cup started a few weeks later). Not wishing to drive all the way to Plymouth and back, I motored to Southampton from Horsham, in West Sussex, where I was living and working and travelled down on the home supporters train.

It was a big game for The Saints who were driving for promotion to the First Division (now called The Premiership). For Plymouth it was a matter of pride, for this was a south coast Derby. The train journey down was an experience in itself. I must have been the only

Argyle supporter on board, surrounded by a sea of red and white-clad Southampton supporters. In those days teams often travelled by train and I recall seeing such legends as Terry Paine, and Jimmy Melia wandering up and down the carriages.

The game itself was a pulsating affair in front of nearly 19,000 fans. Argyle twice took the lead but were well matched by Southampton, who drew level. Then, following a shot from the veteran Melia, a slip-up by Plymouth's goalkeeper, John Leiper (which I can still vividly recall today), saw the ball roll under his body, giving Southampton a three-goals-to-two lead.

Argyle could not get back into the game in the remaining 35 minutes or so and, when the final whistle went a number of joyful Saints supporters invaded the pitch. They were now only one point from promotion with one game to go and duly won it as runners up in the division.

I don't remember much about the train journey back except for a lot of celebrations by the fans in red and white.

Eight months later I took my parents in my white mini, resplendent with my Plymouth Argyle sticker, to Millwall in East London to watch the (unbeaten for 59 home games) Docklanders take on Argyle. The atmosphere at the Den was overpowering from the kick-off, but little did we know that this match would tear up the home team's unbeaten record as Argyle emerged the winners by two goals to one.

Many of the home supporters could not contain their rage at the opposition's shock win. Some Argyle players were attacked as they left the pitch after the final whistle, while others were manhandled as they sought shelter in their dressing room.

We made a quick exit from our seats in the stand, making our way back to the car, unaware that the coach that had brought the West Country team to the ground from Paddington Station had been attacked, and some of its windows smashed and the windscreen damaged. We only learned of the extent of the violence when we read about it in next day's national press, but appreciated that it was down to a minority of Millwall supporters. For us, the unexpected victory was an achievement to be proud of.

As it was 17 years later when, on 14 April 1984, Argyle met Watford (who were managed by Graham Taylor) in the semi-final of the FA Cup at Villa Park in Birmingham.

It was a first for us, and I was lucky enough to get a ticket along with a friend of mine from Bristol, Geoff, who was a long-standing Watford supporter. It was Geoff who left the ground a happy person having seen his team clinch a 1—0 victory over The Pilgrims.

Played in front of nearly 44,000 fans, it was a wonderful occasion and Argyle were by no means the underdogs. In fact they were brilliant and might just have pulled off the shock of the decade if a couple of shots had not just shaved the post.

But Watford's goal, scored just before the game was 15 minutes old, was enough to secure them a visit to Wembley the following month, where they were beaten 2—0 by Everton.

The following season, when watching Argyle play away to Leyton Orient, I came across the journalist and socialist Paul Foot sitting in the away fans' stand. There were not many of us there. It was a miserable, wet October night and we lost 3—0. From then on I was often in his company at away games.

I first met Paul (nephew of Michael Foot) in 1974 when I worked at the International Socialists printing works in East London, where he worked as a reporter for the weekly Socialist Worker. The following season I travelled down to Reading (who were top of Division 3) with Paul and Michael Foot (Paul was driving) to watch the clash between the two clubs at Elm Park.

It was a memorable day. On the drive down Michael talked about the time he heard the one-time leader of the Liberal Party and Prime Minister Lloyd George speak at a public meeting and the electrifying effect he had on listeners. Michael himself was a brilliant public speaker and, of course, a life-time supporter of Plymouth Argyle and MP for Plymouth Devonport for ten years from 1945.

His father took him and his brother to his first match in 1923 when he was eight years old. He remained a passionate supporter right up until his death in 2010 (Paul sadly died six years earlier). If the journey was an amazing experience, so was the game. Argyle were leading 2—0 at half time and within minutes of the restart scored a third. All of us felt confident of a great away victory, even when Reading pulled one goal back through a penalty. How wrong can you be?

In the last ten minutes of the game, Reading scored three goals to end up winners by 4—3.

We were as shocked as some of the Reading supporters were surprised. No triumphal journey back to London but the lively conversation made up for the disappointment.

The next time I met Michael was in May 1996 when Argyle reached the Division 3 play-off final in Wembley against Darlington. Some 22 of us met up in an Italian restaurant near Finchley Road underground station. During lunch I got every member of the party to sign my copy of Harley Lawer's 1988 book *Argyle Classics* which recorded memorable moments in the club's history. (The book's

*Second time around*

foreword was written by Michael.) After the meal and in high spirits we boarded an underground train to Wembley Park. It was a short but eventful journey with many passengers wanting to shake Michael by the hand.

'You're the best Prime Minister we never had,' was one of the many compliments paid to him by complete strangers.

Signing for Argyle

Michael was at ease with all of them. At the stadium, Michael and one or two others departed for the VIP seats while the rest of us made our way to the Argyle section of the stands. That season, we had missed promotion to Division 2 by one point and the 35,000 or so Plymouth fans felt that victory was in our grasp.

They were right, we won the match 1—0, thanks to a fine headed goal by Ronnie Mauge in the second half. We left the stadium in high spirits with pride.

It is a day I will never forget and I still have the match programme.

I returned to Wembley (the 'new' Wembley as it was now) on Saturday 30 May 2016, twenty years after our last appearance at the national stadium, for another play off final, this time against AFC Wimbledon, in the revamped Division 2 (previously Division 4). In that time both Paul and Michael had died and the club had nearly gone bust five years before, but our fan base was still strong.

Whilst Wimbledon home attendances at their Kingston upon Thames ground was just under 5,000, they managed to bring 25,000 supporters to the game. With a total attendance of nearly 58,000 that day, Argyle fans outnumbered those from the south London club, but it was the Dons who won the day. For the first 75 minutes it was a reasonably even, but unexciting game, and although we had the greater possession, we could not make it count.

Wimbledon got the breakthrough in the 78th minute when Lyle Taylor beat our defence and scored from a well-aimed cross. Well into injury time 'The Dons' got a second from a penalty and it was all over.

But for Wimbledon victory was well deserved, not just on the play that day, but because of their remarkable story. It was their sixth promotion since their formation in 2002 by fans of the old Wimbledon FC following their controversial and very unpopular move to Milton Keynes—an achievement against the odds and down to 'fan power' and determination. (Next year they are moving back to Wimbledon from their present temporary home in Kingston, Surrey.)

Two years later we were back in Division 1 (having left it in the 2010/11 season) but last autumn things looked grim. In October we were bottom of the League and looking a likely candidate to return to Division 2 after having just been promoted. The turning point came at the away game at Wimbledon (them again) on 21 October. Despite our poor league position there were over 700 of us willing and cheering Argyle on and we got our reward, a hard-earned 1—0 victory.

*Second time around*

From then on the only way was up and due to a remarkable turn-around we ended the season in seventh position, just three points away from the play offs—a tribute to manager Derek Adams and his hard-working and committed small squad of players. What a season it had been and what a club.

Thanks for the memories, Plymouth Argyle. I'm looking forward to many more and maybe with a strengthened squad, promotion to the second tier next season?

### *Postscript*
(Written 29 December 2019 and 12 August 2020)
My optimism was misplaced. At the end of the season Argyle was relegated to Division 2 and the manager Derek Adams was sacked. So what to look forward to in the 2019/20 season?

A new manager, Ryan Lowe, appointed from financially mismanaged and bankrupted Bury Town FC in Lancashire, who themselves having just been promoted to Division 1 before they hit a financial storm, were expelled from the Football League. With the season at the half-way point, Argyle is seventh in the division, in the play-off zone and with a couple of games in hand over the leaders, but predictions on promotion are unwise.

For me the highlight of 2019 was the naming of the boardroom in the new £8 million-plus Mayflower Grandstand at Home Park, in honour of Jack Leslie, the first black player to be named in the English national team.

John Francis (Jack) Leslie played for Argyle between 1921-1934, a total of 401 games scoring 137 goals. He died in Gravesend, Kent in 1988. © Plymouth Argyle Football Club

The year was 1925, but Jack never kicked a ball for his country. He was one of only two black footballers playing in the Football League at the time. The other, Eddie Patrick, became the first black player to play for Wales in 1931.

Shortly after receiving the news of his selection as a reserve, Jack received a communication cancelling his call-up and, when the squad was formally announced, Billy Walker, of Aston Villa, had taken his place. Jack never again was given the chance to play for his country. It had nothing to do with his footballing skills; he was just the wrong colour for the FA.

In 'Tribute to a Pioneer', 8 December 2019, the Argyle website states:

> Years after the incident, when he was part of the backroom team at West Ham United—his local team—Leslie claimed that: 'They [the selection hierarchy] must have forgotten I was a coloured boy ' as the reason why he was dropped.
>
> He said: 'I did hear, roundabout like, that the FA had come to have another look at me. Not at me football but at me face. They asked, and found they'd made a ricket. Found out about me daddy, and that was it.
>
> 'There was a bit of an uproar in the papers. Folks in the town were very upset. No one ever told me official like but that had to be the reason; me mum was English but me daddy was black as the Ace of Spades. There wasn't any other reason for taking my cap away.'

Simon Hallett, the club's owner is determined that the club should play their part in driving racism and other forms of discrimination out of football in England. He commented: 'One of the club's values is respect, which means that we will do our upmost to eradicate discrimination on any grounds.

'Discrimination on the grounds of race is something that is close to my heart and to my wife's heart and something that my children have been active in trying to fight.'

*https://www.pafc.co.uk/news/2019/december/tribute-to-a-pioneer/*

*Second time around*

# Pandemic

## 65 Profit from pain...
*26 March 2020*

**In the middle of the worst public health crisis in our lifetimes comes some familiar news. There are always some who make a profit out of public adversity.**

So step forward Bill Ackman, a hedge fund manager who according to the Guardian (26 March) has claimed his firm made $2.6bn (£2.2bn) betting that the coronavirus outbreak would cause a market crash. And this barely a week after telling US companies: 'Hell is coming.' It seems that he took advantage of bond market turmoil to make almost 100 times his original outlay of $27m on bets on market movements.

Meanwhile, in the UK, some 5 million self-employed workers are still waiting to hear what kind of financial support they will get. After much delay, a government announcement is expected sometime today.

But it's not just hedge fund managers who are making massive financial windfalls. A few days earlier, the General Medical Council (GMC) raised concerns that some doctors were 'exploiting patients' vulnerability' and making hundreds of thousands of pounds selling private coronavirus tests to people worried that they may have been infected.

The GMC said no doctor should try to 'profit from the fear and uncertainty caused by the pandemic'.

The warning followed reports that Dr Mark Ali of the Private Harley Street Clinic made a £1.7m profit selling £2.5 million-worth of tests in less than a week. The Sunday Times Insight Team claimed in their article *Exposed: the doctor who got £2.5m in a week from 'Coronavirus tests'*, published on 22 March 2020, that Ali boasted to a reporter that he had 'done quite well actually', selling 6,664 tests for £375 each. According to press reports, the tests Ali sold were bought via a third party from testing centre Randox Laboratories, which sells the tests for £120. The tests have not been approved by Public Health England. Ali denied saying he had made £1.7m profit and when approached by the Guardian, he declined to state how much he had made, claiming, the paper reported, that he had been misquoted.

Days before Monday's 'lock down' government announcement it was reported that wealthy families, desperate to escape the coronavirus crisis in London, were fleeing the capital for the country—with some offering up to £50,000-a-month for a rural sanctuary.

British estate agents reported that they have been flooded with requests from the super-rich searching for mansions with bunkers, Cotswolds manor houses and uninhabited Caribbean islands to buy.

The story was highlighted in the Financial Times ('Shortcuts: self-isolating in style' 21/22 March), which reported that clients seeking such retreats have been prepared to double their usual holiday budgets with one booking for a nine-bedroom house in the Home Counties fetching £50,000 per week for a three-months tenure. It also reported that the Landmark Trust, a charity offering holidays in historic buildings, had reported an increase in demand and had taken bookings for the Martello tower, a fort in Aldeburgh, Suffolk with walls more than 2m thick, and the China Tower, also known as the Bicton Belvedere, an octagonal castellated Gothic tower built in 1839 and located on the Rolle estate above the Otter estuary near Sidmouth in Devonshire. The charity emphasises that it has enhanced cleaning at its properties, including the use of virucidal disinfectants. So that's good to know.

Meanwhile, soon to be a backbencher again, Labour leader Jeremy Corbyn tweeted on 24 March that people are waiting for hours on the #UniversalCredit helpline or placed up to 78,000th in an online queue. Cuts of nearly 50,000 staff from the Department for Work and Pensions (DWP) since 2010 have created a system that was failing even before this crisis.

People need financial security if they're expected to stay home when that means they cannot work.

Enough said.

*Second time around*

# Obituaries

## 66  Geraldine Alferoff
*18 August 2016*

**My close friend and comrade Geraldine Alferoff died suddenly at her home in Knighton, Wales on 21 July 2016. We will be celebrating her life at an event in Walthamstow, London E17 on 8 October. Last Friday at her cremation in Hereford I gave the following address:**

The death of Geraldine, someone we know and love, was both shocking and painful, even more so as it was unexpected. We are here today to offer our personal and collective goodbyes to her.

©Barry White

This gathering brings us together to express sadness at our loss but also to celebrate the life she lived and to remember the contribution she made to all our lives.

I wondered just what could I say to express my feelings as someone who knew her from the time she joined Nalgo (the public sector white collar union) as a publicity field organiser in 1983, I think it was, and worked with her along with other colleagues who are also here today, until I left UNISON, as it was then called, in 1997.

I continued to keep in touch with her when she left Walthamstow to move to Knighton with her family in 2006.

On this occasion words don't seem enough, but words are perhaps the only way we have of expressing ourselves. So I am reminded of a passage in a book *Some Lives* written by the late Dave Widgery, a socialist and a doctor who lived and died in the East End of London. In the chapter 'Not Going Gently', which deals with loss, such as we are faced with today Dave wrote:

How few deaths are 'acceptable'. I was angry and hurt even when a ninety-six-year-old friend died. Indeed you can get lost in a pit of grief, determining you will never laugh or dance or joke again. But humans are enormously adaptable, have ways of healing their mental as well as physical pain. It's not the passage of time that matters, however, but what you do with it. Only with efforts do we extract from the irreplaceable something that falls into place...

Geraldine would not want us to get lost in a pit of grief as Dave Widgery called it. When I came to stay with her and her family in early June she was talking about how she could get the local Labour Party, which she had joined along with many others following the election last year of Jeremy Corbyn as leader, campaigning around local issues that would improve people's lives. She would say in words well known to many of us: Don't mourn, organise.

Geraldine has died but she still lives on in our hearts and minds. She is loved, her life valued and she will never be forgotten.

## 67 Chris Bartter

*8 January 2018*

**Chris Bartter, socialist, journalist, trade unionist and campaigner, died on 28 October aged 64 from a heart attack.**

I first met Chris in the 1980s when I was a publicity field organiser for Nalgo (now UNISON) and he was a lay publicity activist and campaigner in Scotland.

Scotland was his adopted home. Chris, always larger than life, was born in north London and then moved to Dorking in Surrey before moving on to Glasgow to study at Strathclyde University. In 1975 he went to work at the Mitchell

Library, now one of Europe's largest public libraries. There he joined the public service union Nalgo and met his partner Doreen.

*Second time around*

Chris moved from being a leading publicity and campaigning activist to become the union's first full-time communications organiser in Scotland, where he inspired and trained many lay activists in both publicity and campaigning skills. He also had great organising skills, chairing the 7.84 theatre company, building Glasgow's May Day as a city wide trade union festival and, following his retirement from UNISON, helping launch the Nelson Mandela Scottish Memorial Foundation and the Havana-Glasgow Film Festival.

Chris was a regular contributor to the Morning Star, where he wrote for the cultural pages. He was also a tireless campaigner for the Scottish Freedom of Information Campaign. But it was not a solo act: Doreen, who survives him, was also his partner in his political and campaigning work.

Chris was a kind person with a great sense of humour. He is sorely missed not only by his army of friends but by all who came into contact with him, many of who turned out to his funeral in Glasgow on 13 November.

But the greatest loss will be felt by his partner Doreen and his sister Vanessa. His life has been an inspiration for the many, and he will live on in our hearts and minds.

# Climate change

## 68 We have been warned ... again and again

*16 September 2020*

**According to some press reports, BBC One's screening on 14 September of Sir David Attenborough's new documentary *Extinction: The Facts* left many viewers shocked, terrified and angry.**

The hour-long programme saw the legendary natural historian and fellow experts investigate the devastating effects of climate change and habitat loss on wildlife and plant life, and how it's also impacting humanity and the planet.

Disturbing scenes showed the details of how a million different species are at risk of extinction in a biodiversity crisis that is also putting us all at greater risk of pandemic diseases like Covid-19.

Watching the programme, it was tempting to say, 'Well that's it, there is nothing we can do, it's all over.'

Attenborough, however, would not agree. He concluded the programme on a positive note: 'I do truly believe that, together, we can create a better future. I might not be here to see it, but if we make the right decisions at this critical moment, we can safeguard our planet's ecosystems, its extraordinary biodiversity and all its inhabitants. What happens next is up to every one of us.'

Meanwhile, according to the charity World Wildlife Fund (WWF), in one of the world's most comprehensive examinations of biodiversity on our planet (*Living Planet Report 2020: Bending the Curve of Biodiversity Loss\**), the natural world is in a 'desperate' state, with global wildlife populations 'in freefall' as a result of human activity. Hammering home Sir David Attenborough's message, the charity paints a startlingly bleak picture of the rapid damage being wrought by modern civilisation, warning that 'nature is being destroyed by humans at a rate never seen before, and this catastrophic decline is showing no signs of slowing.'

The report says that populations of mammals, birds, fish, amphibians and reptiles have collapsed by an extraordinary 68 per cent on average globally since 1970—more than two thirds in 50 years.

It also finds that intensive agriculture, deforestation and the conversion of wild spaces into farmland are among the main drivers of natural destruction, while overfishing is 'wreaking havoc with marine life'.

It wonders if everything we've seen in 2020 is enough to make us reset our relationship with nature and points out that we know what needs to be done if we're to have a chance of putting nature on a path to recovery by 2030. Like Sir David Attenborough, the report strikes a positive note, pointing out that with global action to protect wildlife, produce food in better ways, and change what we choose to eat, we can turn things around.

Both *Extinction: The Facts* and the WWF report make it absolutely clear about the stark choices and consequences before us. As the report concludes: 'Citizens, governments and business leaders around the globe will need to be part of a movement for change with a scale, urgency and ambition never seen before.'

However, the views of those who say that the very economic system, capitalism, that has landed us in this crisis is just not capable of getting us out, need to be taken seriously.

Writing in the Guardian on 18 March 2019 ('Ending climate change requires the end of capitalism. Have we got the stomach for it?'), Phil McDuff states: 'the existing political establishment looks more and more like an impediment to change. The consequences of global warming have moved from the merely theoretical and predicted to observable reality over the past few years, but this has not been matched by an uptick in urgency. The need to keep the wheels of capitalism well-oiled takes precedence even against a backdrop of fires, floods and hurricanes.'

A year ago Extinction Rebellion started an online bust-up by tweeting, 'We are not a socialist movement.'

Some say environmentalism without socialism is just gardening. But does it need to be that way? Is socialism the only way for the climate movement to make progress? Or will that limit its appeal? Are sections of the climate movement making a mistake by aligning just with the left?

These questions are not yet the subject of mainstream discussion in the climate movement. Surely as the continuing failures of governments and capitalism to actually get to grips with the crisis, including by taking action against companies responsible for the devastating effects of climate change, become more apparent, such questions will move to the centre of the debate and must be answered.

Yet, speaking of capitalism, Alice Ross (Financial Times) in her recent book *Investing to Save the Planet*, shows how some big businesses are waking up to the fact that climate change will have a negative effect on their future profits and is becoming an increasing financial risk.

It's worth recalling that five years earlier in a landmark speech called 'Breaking the tragedy of the horizon—climate change and financial stability', to the insurance market Lloyd's of London, Mark Carney, then governor of the Bank of England, explained that 'Climate change is the tragedy of the horizon' and that 'once climate change becomes a defining issue for financial stability, it may already be too late.'

Indeed it already may be.

\* *https://www.wwf.org.uk/sites/default/files/2020-09/LPR20_Full_report.pdf*

# Acknowledgements

The author and publishers would like to thank the following for permission to use their material

## Photographs

### *Front cover*
The author being interviewed outside the Instanbul Çağlayan Justice Palace (the largest courthouse in Europe and the scene of many journalists' trials): picture from the European Federation of Journalists

### *Back cover*
The author with colleagues from the Journalists Union of Turkey Türkiye Gazeteciler Sendikasi (TGS) at their Istanbul offices: picture from TGS

*We have tried to contact all copyright holders asking for permission to quote material from their publications. If we have inadvertently used material for which permission should have been granted, please contact us.*